This is my stream of consciousness
— of words and images — inspired
by Fremantle. There are
thousands of others …

Fremantle IMPRESSIONS

RON DAVIDSON

FREMANTLE ARTS CENTRE PRESS

NO ENTRY

A meander around Fremantle in search of its stories and snapshots begins on Manjaree — Arthur Head — the diminished but still impressive limestone cliff that has seen it all.

It saw the Wagyl rest after creating the Swan River; it saw trade fairs with Nyungars exchanging goods over thousands of years and feasting on roasted meat carved from an occasional beached whale; and in 1829 it saw Captain Fremantle hoisting the British flag over what the King had proclaimed 'uninhabited territory'. It saw the apparatus of authority and defence built there, and Yagan, resistance fighter or outlaw, casually joke with his former gaoler at the Round House. It watched a restrained Georgian village become in ten years a town dripping with Gold Rush extravagance, and saw the very limestone from which it is formed used to build C Y O'Connor's South Mole. Arthur Head has also seen four or five wars pass by, and an America's Cup defence which is a sort of war; it may almost have glimpsed footballer John Gerovich's soaring marks, somewhere to the east. It surely saw a slender Sicilian boy arrive at Victoria Quay, a boy who would defy the flies and turn Fremantle's dining al fresco.

Picture Lionel Samson and his younger brother William arriving by lighter at Anglesea Point, just south of Arthur Head, on 5 August 1829. The immigrant ship they sailed on, *Calista*, is standing off Bathers Beach, Fremantle, as they scan the Swan River Colony, now just two months old. The constant north-westerly gale whips sand and spray over the assortment of inappropriate tools and unsuitable clothing and furniture now littering the beach. There's water everywhere: the Indian Ocean and the Swan River; a freshwater spring and a string of oval-shaped brackish ponds cut off a small triangle of land which has Arthur Head as its apex. The ponds are home to ducks who patiently wait to be shot.

It's cold: in three months there'll be heat, flies, scurvy and dysentery, and some adjacent Nyungar bush firings which the settlers find alarming. They've come to give their prospects a boost in Governor Stirling's Garden of Eden and shelter in tents which frequently catch fire, or in brush huts, or in caves in the headland whose limestone ridges and large dunes curve

Horace Samson, 'View of the Tunnel under the Round House and the Whaling Jetty at Fremantle', c1840.

[Fremantle City Library: Local History Collection]

Frontispiece: Heavy lifter heads for Hong Kong with two Austal ferries, with the Maritime Museum immediately behind and Fremantle Prison in the distance, 2003.

[Photo Moderne]

Previous Page: The return of the verandahs, High Street, 2003.

[Michal Lewi]

The original Samson building, and Fanny's Cottage to the left, 1895.
[Fremantle City Library: Local History Collection]

around the bay. There's even a horse house, but the magnificent horse which should have pulled it up the beach is dead from severe bruising inflicted during storms in the Indian Ocean. Some women and children sleep in the rain, 'protected' only by an occasional parasol or an empty champagne crate. John Bateman II arrives there a little later. He's only seven and will quickly become one of Fremantle's most adventurous whalers and then a major merchant, but in his early weeks on the beach he has to shelter in a broken vinegar barrel. Fremantle is proving a hard place defined by a large rock.

The Samsons are different from most new arrivals. They don't need to make a fortune: they already have a considerable one. Lionel, at twenty-eight, has a seat on the London Stock Exchange and the family is well connected with financiers like the Rothschilds and the Levis. King George IV, who has proclaimed this 'uninhabited territory' for the British Crown, puts on a farewell grouse shoot for the brothers before they sail for Fremantle. Their arrival is about adventure and challenge and escape from the 'increasing boredom' of London's financial district.

The Oxford-educated adventurers do not despair at the lack of preparation that greets them. They organise their substantial cargo of wine, spirits and groceries, and within days their shop on the beach is doing good business. What will become — and

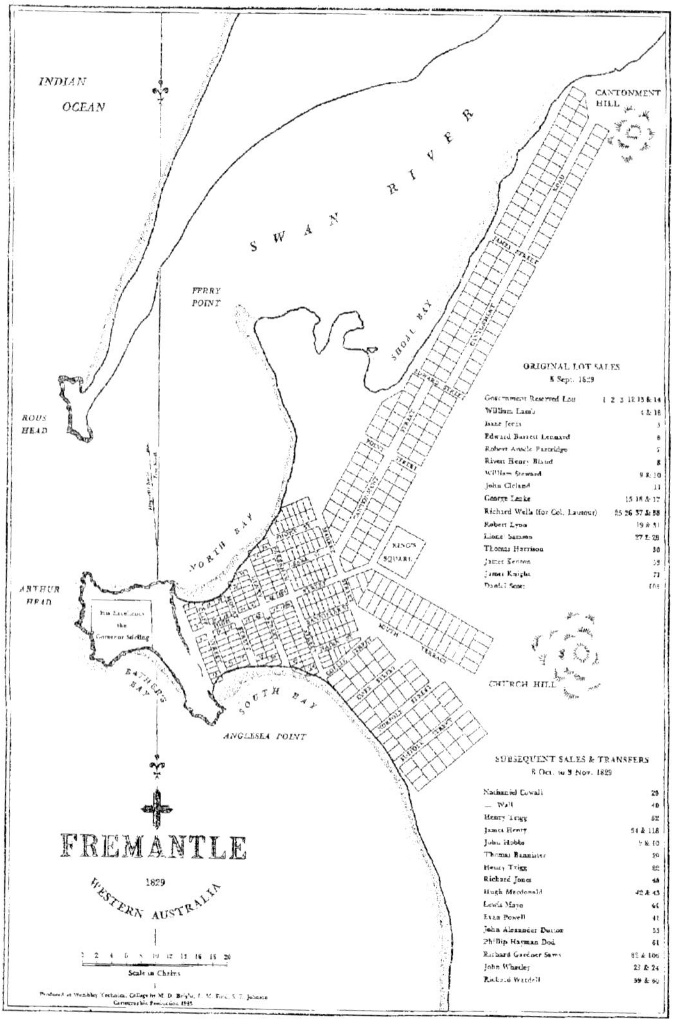

J S Roe's first town plan for Fremantle, 1830.
[Fremantle City Library: Local History Collection]

is still — Australia's oldest family company is afloat, although the colony looks like sinking around it. But John Septimus Roe speedily prepares a town plan which at many points incorporates indigenous pathways. Shifting sand becomes real estate and, in September, the brothers buy a block of land in Cliff Street at the colony's first land sale. Soon their company is operating from a basic limestone cottage on the site of what is now the richly detailed company headquarters at Number 31. Lionel becomes Fremantle's first postmaster-general. It is not a lucrative position. In fact he's not paid at all and has to meet the costs of taking the mail halfway to Perth. Also, the settlers lack funds to pay for postage due on their letters. Lionel lends money to them and that is not all. Soon he is providing settlers with a free tot of rum to lift their spirits while they wait till the boat comes in. Lionel can afford to wait for better times. And he does get his mail first.

After initially following the British tradition and depositing their prisoners in the storm-wrecked *Marquis of Anglesea,* in 1830 Australia's first colony of freemen begins work on Fremantle Gaol, later known as the Round House. It is designed by Henry Reveley, a civil engineer who has already completed a sea wall and small jetty just south of Arthur Head. His father is Willey 'Greek' Reveley, one of the leaders of the classical revival movement in English architecture, and some say the son's prison design reflects elements of the father. Fremantle historian David Hutchison gives me an alternative explanation: Henry spent time sailing in Italy where he once rescued his friend, poet and insatiable sailor, Percy Bysshe Shelley, from drowning. The Fremantle building may be influenced by the bare and exposed coastal forts Reveley encountered in Italy.

Shackled to a wall in Reveley's Fremantle Gaol — the Roundhouse — during October 1832 is the Aboriginal leader Yagan, and two of his friends. Yagan has been declared an outlaw after a deadly reprisal raid following the death of his friend who was shot while raiding a settler's potato patch near Fremantle. He has a £20 bounty on his head. Some settlers view Yagan as the noble savage par excellence. Most still fear him. Robert Menli Lyon is a sensitive protector of the Indigenous population. He is a Scot and sees them as similar to the ancient Caledonians: simple and generous. Yagan is a prince, like William Wallace, the thirteenth century resistance leader. Lyon believes he can 'civilise' Yagan by Christianising him and then, he believes, other Aborigines will follow. Soon the participants in this social experiment, including a number of soldiers, are sailing for Carnac, a treeless windswept island half a kilometre across and twelve kilometres offshore. Carnac is the home of a substantial population of tiger snakes who feed on seagull eggs

Fremantle artist, Brian McKay and the Round House at sunset, 1994. Brian McKay produced an iconic series of paintings of the site in the mid-1980s.
[Brad Rimmer]

Charles Dirk Wittenoom, 'View from the Court House, Arthur Head, Fremantle', c1838.

[Fremantle City Library: Local History Collection]

and chicks. There is little else, apart from fish. After six weeks Yagan, freed of his chains, tires of spearing reef fish and helping Lyon record the languages and the geography of local tribes. Lyon believes he sees Yagan kneeling and praying. He rejoices. Yagan and his friends steal a dinghy and row to the mainland. The colonists are baffled. How can these simple people row without specific lessons? Lyon is devastated by this duplicity.

Yagan appears around the sandy waste which is Cliff Street. For thousands of years it has been a well-walked pathway between sea and river and a popular meeting place in spring and summer. No-one tries to apprehend him for eight months. He dances at a corroboree attended by leading settlers. Still no-one makes a move. The *Perth Gazette* is impressed: 'Yagan was the master of ceremonies and acquitted himself with infinite dignity and grace.' Later the newspaper notes, with approval, how he calls on his former gaoler one evening, points to the gaol door, then towards Carnac. He chuckles at his own joke. Meanwhile, the Murray River leader, Calyute, is taken to the Round House after a spectacular raid on the flour mill in South Perth. Neville Green writes that each night Calyute's people creep up to the Prison walls and call to him softly. Soon other Aborigines are coming at night to visit their relatives at Fremantle Gaol waiting to be shipped to more permanent confinement on Rottnest, the Aborigines' gulag. Calyute is given sixty lashes and released.

Swan river-mouth, showing Cliff Street river jetty and Ferry Point where Nyungars crossed, c1890.
[Fremantle Ports]

Arthur Head is where other meetings between Nyungar and colonist take place. Some are hostile. In 1833 Yagan's brother Domjum dies after being shot while climbing into a food store at the ocean end of Cliff Street. The strength of the Aboriginal notion of a mutual sharing of resources is poorly appreciated by the less sensitive of the settlers. This store has been closed following the death by shooting of its owner, the merchant George French Johnson, in what was thought to be the colony's only duel, but there are now doubts about this. Payback for Domjum's death is quick and savage: the price on Yagan's head goes up to £30. He is wanted dead or alive and now wears an English military jacket under his traditional kangaroo-skin cape. He hopes this will cover the distinctive tribal marking extending across his shoulders, which makes him too ready a target. But no-one moves to apprehend him. His meetings with the more literate settlers are heavy with foreboding. Finally, in July 1833, he is shot by a young bounty hunter he has befriended in the Upper Swan region. Yagan's head is hacked off, smoked in a hollow log, then shipped to Britain. His skin with its distinctive marking is another trophy. The bounty hunter is speared to death. George Fletcher Moore, the literate solicitor and colonial administrator, feels the story has all the characteristics of a Greek tragedy: Yagan's tempestuous nature brings inevitable calamity.

Actor David Gulpilil, another imperious black, dances one warm evening in the summer of 1986–87 with the Round House as his backdrop. He seems about to float off the rock. Instead he plants his feet in the grass. 'More! More!' demand the America's Cup audience. David Gulpilil doesn't dance. Instead, he confronts his audience.

'More what?'

'More, please.' With just the suggestion of disdain he floats again.

Cliff Street consolidates with wattle and daub, timber and, among the wealthier, ballast brick and dry-limestone houses and stores. Fremantle has about a hundred such houses by 1836. Many remain unfinished and some are already being covered with sand. Having lost their fragile cover of vegetation, the dunes are on the move. Despite this, Cliff Street is still the shortest path between the ocean and river jetties, and the centre of activity for as long as a limestone bar and shallows block the mouth of the Swan River.

'Our colony is built on a beach,' writes George Fletcher Moore in his diary. He reports that 'the colonists are a cheerless, dissatisfied people with gloomy looks, who plod through the sand from hut to hut, to drink grog and grumble.' Jane Roberts, an early visitor and writer, reports, 'the ladies

David Gulpilil
dances — like Yagan.
[National Archives of Australia: A6180 3/2/82/1]

employed themselves as well as the heat would allow with books, work and the occasional sketching', but she complains of problems at night. 'The buzz or sting of musquitoes [sic], the constant snapping noise of the lizards, with the feeling of very close and disagreeable contact were the annoyances of the night.' Presumably that annoying contact was human, given Mary Ann Friend's complaint about soldiers singing and drinking in nearby tents. Mary Ann adds: 'We expected to find land but only found sand.' Nearly a hundred and fifty years later, newspaper columnist Bernie Kirwan Ward wonders at what point 'these whingeing Poms become noble pioneers'. He suggests that historians should try to answer his question.

Yagan's father Midgegooroo is killed by a firing squad in a quasi-legal execution some months before his son's murder. It is 1844 before the colony's first execution of a non-Aborigine takes place at the crossroads, near where Cliff and High Streets intersect. John Gavin, aged about fifteen and a thief, has come with other boys from Britain's Parkhurst Reformatory for rehabilitation in the colony. Sent between 1842 and 1849, they are arguably Fremantle's first convicts. John is charged with murdering his employer's son with an axe 'in an uncontrollable outburst of anger'. He is sentenced to death on Holy Thursday: he can't be hanged on Good Friday but it's all right on Easter Saturday. Gavin is wearing new shoes on the short walk from

Cliff Street grows.
Detail from lithograph of Charles Dirk Wittenoom's, View from the Court House, Arthur Head, Fremantle, *c1838.*
[Fremantle City Library: Local History Collection]

The original St John's church looks down High Street at the original Fremantle Gaol, c1845.
[S M Stout; The Battye Library — 5770B/34]

Following page: Well-dressed settlers near Fremantle row into town to do some shopping, whilst their cow finds the grass on the other side of the fence, c1890.
[Beatel and Williams]

the gaol. He removes them in case they get damaged. Gavin is a slender lad and is wrapped in chains, presumably to ensure the drop will break his neck as the horse and cart is whipped away; which it does. The hangman is praised for his compassion. The body is taken away to allow a plaster mould of Gavin's head to be made as Fremantle's contribution to the popular notions of phrenology and the 'criminal mind'. He is then buried in a sand dune south of Arthur Head. Women are also being imprisoned at the Round House. The year John Gavin is hanged Susan Hitchcock, unmarried, is gaoled for one year for stealing items of her mistress's finery: she wants to dress like a lady. While in gaol her baby arrives — stillborn. At the eastern end of High Street, facing the gibbet and the original Fremantle Gaol, is the first Anglican church, St John's.

Meander along Cliff Street. George Fletcher Moore lived here in the early 1830s but it's not clear quite where. He is amazed his vegetables grow in his garden of sand. The two-storey limestone cottage on Cliff Street once housed his entrepreneurial nephew, William Dalgety Moore. It still looks snug behind the Fremantle Hotel, built over Moore's front garden, which also flourished in the sand. The quartermaster on the *Beagle* also has something to say about the sand around Cliff Street: he could run the whole settlement through an hourglass inside twenty-four hours.

Life is improving for some Fremantle settlers, with advances in farming, whaling and sandalwood cutting, but the servants are revolting. A number of them are battered remnants of the Battle of Waterloo; one of them, William Adams, advertises himself around Fremantle as the Hero of Waterloo and talks about his head wound. He may also be the progenitor of the celebrated Fremantle tradition of storytelling, but settlers take little notice. When his grave is dug up — as the Skinner Street Cemetery is cleared to make space for John Curtin High School's playing fields — a silver skull-plate falls from the shovel. At least that part of his story is true. Meanwhile William's wife Elizabeth sets up as the first of a celebrated line of Fremantle midwives which includes Nurse Sheedy, grandmother of Jack Sheedy, football hero. Elizabeth Evans is called the Mother of Fremantle and claims to have 'never lost a case'. The Mother of Fremantle has twelve children of her own.

Fremantle attracts a number of indentured recruits from the parish poorhouses in the south of England. Some look for new jobs. A few are on their way to becoming merchants; others display an in-your-face attitude and many quickly die of dysentery and scurvy. Others, according to records from Fremantle's first public cemetery in Alma Street, have more bizarre exits. William Carpenter dies of a 'visitation by God', William Sutton goes 'silly and is found dead with his head in

The Adams family in Fremantle: William, Elizabeth and grand-daughter Mary Ann, c1863.
[Fremantle City Library: Local History Collection]

a waterhole' and Cecil John dies of 'hard living'. Mr John is not alone in this regard.

The Masters can meet any challenge from the Servants by giving them a spell in the wreck, *Anglesea,* then later in Fremantle Gaol, courtesy of the *Masters and Servants Act.* Stocks are even erected on Arthur Head, at a time when they are being abolished elsewhere. The Servants have a significant win in the winter of 1839 when a north-wester blows three ships ashore from their anchorage in Gage Roads. They don't re-float them until guaranteed a payment of twelve shillings a day. Despite this early stand, it will be fifty years before Fremantle's first maritime union is established.

Keep walking north along old Cliff Street past the Fremantle Hotel and Moore's cottage to the Elder building which replaced George Shenton's opulent residence during the building boom around 1900. It's now Barwil House and also carries the name Wilhelmsen. The building, with its fine detail on a domed corner tower is, says the conservation report, 'a fulcrum about which the surrounding buildings are in balance'. Take a look through the Cliff Street entrance at the building's remarkable cedar joinery, complex jarrah staircase, white marble floor and pressed iron ceilings. There's also a grand business chamber, all designed by Talbot Hobbs, the Englishman whose first job in Australia is constructing seats at

The unhappy paintwork of the Elder building now reduces the drama of the exterior, but the interiors are still imposing.
[Michal Lewi]

the original Fremantle train station nearby, at the river end of Cliff Street. Hobbs becomes the architect of many of Fremantle's landmark buildings, including the Scots Church in South Terrace, now the Chinese Presbyterian Church, and the Park Hotel, which now houses the aged and unfortunate. As a part-time soldier, then an ageing colonel at Gallipoli and a creative general with Monash in France, 'Little Hobbs' becomes something of a landmark himself.

Now take a sweep across what was once called Phillimore Square, but is quite unsquare. The buildings on the southern end follow the serpentine high-water mark of the Swan River, indicated now by marker bricks set in the pavement. By the time C Y O'Connor's harbour, controversially sited in the river mouth, is opened in 1897, more than fifty acres have been reclaimed to the west. Over the next decade Phillimore Place is completed, with imposing buildings along this new land.

It is easy to see that Phillimore Place is the shippers' confident response to the opening of the inner harbour which, as the historian J S Battye puts it, allows Fremantle to 'leap at a bound from a coastal to an international port'. The international mail boat companies like Peninsular and Orient move up from Albany and position themselves along Phillimore Street which is the main entrance to the new harbour. Four

Phillimore Place, a surprise around every corner, 1970s.
[Michal Lewi]

A customer at the freight section McIlwraith & McEachern Company, 1919.
[Fremantle City Library: Local History Collection]

Not much has changed in 2003 when it is a metallurgist's office.
[Michal Lewi]

grand hotels open in the same year as the harbour. The Yilgarn and the Kalgoorlie gold strikes, along with a safe harbour, boost the struggling Fremantle of 1890 into a boom-town. Wander around the shippers' buildings: many architects and many styles and materials — brick, brick and stucco or less frequently local limestone — but always coherent and with a hard edge to the pavement. There's His Majesty's Hotel (built 1897), Phillimore Chambers (1899), Dock Buildings and the P and O Building (both 1903), combining with the old Customs House to produce a turn-of-the-century streetscape. Look at the elegant arcading of Scottish House, constructed from Donnybrook stone. The interior is even more impressive with compartments for clerks defined by fine joinery, coloured art glass, and a strong hint of Dickens. This is an outstanding building in one of Australia's finest built spaces.

I receive my first lesson on Fremantle society here. My dad, Frank Davidson, alternating between gentle family man and impatient newspaper editor, is driving along Phillimore Street. It is 1948 and I am an unknowing kid. Dad brakes sharply. Four men saunter in front of our small Morris tourer. They are wearing the uniform of the Fremantle lumper: felt hats and serge pants, with cargo hooks hanging from their heavy leather belts. Each carries a Gladstone bag and a large billy. At least I think they do … Or are the evocative photographs of the wharf and its workers by 'Fremantle photographer' Abraham 'Izzy' Orloff obtruding on my consciousness? Or perhaps the doubt stems from auctioneer and bush poet Kevin 'Rusty' Christensen telling me that in the thirties he knows what cargo his lumper-father will be unloading that morning by the hook he thrusts under his belt as he steps out of the door, heading for his bike. A two-pronger says bagged wheat. Later Rusty learns other things about thriving as a youth from Fremantle: when the father of a prospective girlfriend from outside Freo asks where you live, you look him in the eye and reply, 'Mosman Park.'

'Give them a honk, Dad,' I suggest helpfully as the men in front of us show no sign of accelerating; they may even be slowing. 'You don't honk Fremantle people,' says my dad. I don't understand why this should be but don't ask. I am just a kid from South Perth and do not understand that the attitudes embedded in Fremantle people are often hostile to those held in Perth, the foreign province eighteen kilometres upriver. Perceived grievances run deep and have been eating away at residents since 1829.

Even when various attempts are being promoted from Perth to blast away the limestone bar which blocks the entrance to the Swan River and improve the hazardous port facilities, some Fremantle residents are uneasy. Perhaps this is a Perth plot to

Fremantle lumpers, the forklifts of the 1920s.
[A Orloff]

allow ships to bypass Fremantle and sail on to Perth. There are also less severe irritations. The early Perth cricketers are critical of undulations in the Fremantle Green, the slightly wet, grassy land reclaimed by busy bees in the 1840s, at the river end of Mouat and Cliff Streets. But all is forgotten when a considerable crowd of 'ladies and gentlemen' gather to see Fremantle's Lionel Samson beat solicitor George Leake from Perth at single wicket cricket. The press reports the 'dejeuner was excellent'. One hundred and fifty years later, at His Lordship's Larder in the old His Majesty's, just fifty metres from the old pitch, Mick Vodanovich's lunch of corned beef and onions and Khaki Beer, brewed in the hotel, is also excellent. Khaki Beer? That's its colour.

Conflict with Perth is serious on 4 May 1919. Premier Colebatch and a volunteer group including commercial travellers come from Perth in two launches to help build barricades to allow the 'scab union' (the National Workers Union) members to unload the interstate trader *Dimboola.* The Lumpers' Union claims the *Dimboola* has not been adequately quarantined to protect the community from the deadly Spanish influenza pandemic which is sweeping the postwar world. The Nationals, after early solidarity with the Lumpers' Union, want to start work. The Lumpers are determined to stop them.

Hilda Hyde, whose father runs the original Italianate Swan

Victoria Quay is created by dredging, 1893.
[The Battye Library — BA1116/10]

Controversial union leader, politician and embezzler, Fred Baglin addresses a crowd on the Fremantle Esplanade after Bloody Sunday. The crowd votes overwhelmingly to throw into the harbour the barricades erected to keep out members of the Lumpers' Union, 1919.
[Fremantle City Library: Local History Collection]

Hotel, just north of the traffic bridge, watches from the hotel's elegant southern verandah as preliminaries to the Bloody Sunday Riot are fought. Hilda sees scores of women, carrying large rocks and lumps of iron, run onto the bridge as the Premier's launches pass underneath. They bombard them. Four men stagger across the bridge with a large slab of limestone which they balance on the bridge rail then release it. They do not score the direct hit which could sink the launch. Surprisingly, no-one is seriously hurt but Premier Colebatch's biographer (his son) says this was an assassination attempt. Many in Perth are frightened by the news of rocks thudding on a premier's launch and the violent riot which follows. Not so John Curtin, later federal parliamentary member for Fremantle and Second World War prime minister, but then the rabble-rousing editor of the *Westralian Worker* who also ran socialist sunday schools around Fremantle. He defends his comrades on page one under the heading:

> *COLEBATCH THE BLOOD SPILLER*
>
> *There are voices in the land whispering that the Lumpers at Fremantle are a lawless band of rebels. The accusation is a monstrous lie. It was the Premier himself, in his capacity as the cat's-paw of the Shipping Ring, who broke the law by organising a brutal force to accomplish by sheer weight of*

intimidation and armed might the purposes the Shipping Ring nourish at their bosom.

You enter the port proper from Cliff Street. This is where the *West Australian* focuses in its reports on the 'sanguinary aspects' of the clash, which has a total of two thousand lumpers, their families and supporters — some prompted by urging from a Catholic priest at Mass — surging into the port on Bloody Sunday to confront police who are armed with fixed bayonets. Lumper Tom Edwards is hit with a police rifle butt while shielding the fallen Fremantle Lumpers' Union president, Bill Renton, between B and C sheds. The scene becomes even more ugly when a returned soldier is bayoneted. The Riot Act is read and a section of armed police riflemen face the enraged crowd. A bloodbath seems certain but precisely what happens next depends on who you talk to.

Old timers say — or said — Inspector William Sellenger, the senior police officer in Fremantle, and Alex McCallum, the secretary of the State Labour Federation who is not known for his tact, dramatically step from their respective groups and negotiate a temporary settlement. The *West Australian* has Sellenger walking over to the rioters, asking them to 'be quiet' for ten minutes. In the ten minutes of 'quiet' a deal is struck between all parties including Premier Colebatch who

Tom Edwards' cortege leaves for Fremantle Cemetery — and legendary status. The domed Esplanade Hotel, then Daniel Scott's warehouse further to the right, provide a backdrop.
[A Orloff]

All dressed up: Inspector William Sellenger and sons, c1910.
[Western Australian Police Department]

guarantees no Nationals or volunteers will step onto the wharf that day. The deal is done the day Tom Edwards dies of his wounds in Fremantle Hospital, an agreement preserved until the Patrick's cargo-handling dispute seventy years later.

Sellenger has been the hero of many stand-offs at the port. Some say he is too even handed. He is a Fremantle boy; the son of a convict sentenced to fifteen years' transportation to Fremantle when only thirteen. The son is known around Fremantle as the Great White Chief. He is not a big man. Presumably the title comes from his time stationed in Aboriginal areas where he was known as Big Chief White Man because of this even-handedness. After nine years in charge of policing in Fremantle, which can occasionally be like sitting on a powder keg, Sellenger is moved to Bunbury. Commissioner Robert Connell (yes, the grandfather of WA Inc principal Laurie Connell) wants him to have a 'a quieter life'. He is recalled in 1925 when quiet seems to have been restored in Fremantle — just in time for the national seamen's strike which means more aggravation. Then the world-wide British seamen's strike also comes to Fremantle.

You are now walking past the red bricks and heavy slabs of Donnybrook sandstone of the Old Customs House which closed in 1986. It is built in the Federation Free style and oozes

Old Customs House, c1912.
[Fremantle City Library: Local History Collection]

Following page: An express messenger pauses for a feed and read, 1964.
[Fremantle Ports]

authority. Chains still hang from the pressed tin ceiling. These once held signboards above officers' tables showing newcomers where they have to present themselves. But things change. The building becomes Deckchair Theatre and is now Bizircus, an anarchic professional circus group: acrobats and clowns come from France, Russia, China, Africa and Britain to train the troupe which remains assertively Australian. Circus ropes and trapeze swings hang through the light-well. Upstairs are twenty artists' studios administered by the state government's Artsource and housing a range of visual and other artists. Fremantle's poet laureate ('Ode to my Bicycle') Mark Reid works in one of them. He talks of stormy nights in the Customs House. The west winds, which ships' masters in South Bay feared, make the roofing iron bang; doors and windows rattle; and, Mark says, the heavy limestone walls groan. Painters and performers say they have heard ghosts; some see them.

The Customs House is near where the Bloody Sunday rioters enter Victoria Quay and where the bullring operated. A foreman from the stevedoring company stands, sometimes on a box, encircled by men in flannelette shirts. He selects first those who can work for twenty hours at a stretch lumping cargo, who are known to be compliant, and possibly willing to provide a kickback for their benefactor afterwards at the Terminus (previously Pearlers) Hotel. There are also hundreds of casual

PORT AUTHORITY
EXPRESS MESSENGER

jobs around the harbour. Now Paddy Troy's dockies — there are no dockers — toe the chalk line at the corner of Cliff Street. The foreman blows his whistle: they race as best they can. Those who get to the foreman first are employed. The old and the slow miss out and return to the starting line or go home hungry. In the late thirties separate yards are built beside the weighbridge. Here the lumpers and dockies gather, hoping to catch the foreman's eye. In the words of an anonymous poet:

In the cattle yard, down on the wharf
Where only the 'bulls' can get a go,
There isn't a chance to get picked up,
Unless you're in the know.
The pick-up bloke comes to the fence
And as he does the mob commence
To shove and push like hungry cattle;
When not picked up begin to battle.

Look at the uncomplicated cargo sheds. C is the oldest and most complete. It was built in 1903–04 with a gentle curve to match the contours of the wharf. Stand on the narrow strip of bitumen and railway tracks between the sheds and the water; you can still sense crowds and tears and the streamers which several times a week attach those 'going home' to the UK to

Heading for the war; a troup convoy off Fremantle, c1940.
[Australian War Memorial]

Previous page: Fremantle harbour crowded with a motley collection of ships, 1942.
[Saxon Fogarty]

those returning to their homes here. The feeling is a remnant of more than a hundred years of greetings and farewells and the compost of spilled cargoes at Australia's first and last port of call.

Ships carrying troops to and from four wars — is it now five? — come and go. A convoy of the world's great liners carrying Australian, American and New Zealand troops fills Fremantle Harbour on the morning of 10 May 1940. *Empress of Britain* (42,348 old tons), *Empress of Japan* (26,032), *Andes* (25,689), *Mauretania* (35,739) and *Empress of Canada* (21,517) all steam in accompanied by their cruiser escorts *Australia*, *Canberra* and *Leander*. The *Queen Mary* (81,255) and the *Aquitania* (44,786) are waiting, tossing in the deeper water of Gage Roads.

But the Second World War really arrives at Fremantle in November 1941 when the Royal Australian Navy's glamour ship, the battle cruiser *Sydney*, mysteriously fails to return from routine escort duty near Carnarvon. Two months later the port is crowded and chaotic. Ships of all types arrive, fleeing the Japanese onslaught to the north. The city is blacked out and can be a brutal place, except for the kids who swim from Arthur Head to the Southern Slipway where, later, American submariners throw them slices of watermelon.

March 1942 — there are strikes unlike any others. A dispute between Chinese crew and British masters on China

Navigation freighters has three hundred Australian soldiers swarming on to the *Chungking* and *Hanyang* which are double-banked alongside North Wharf. Troops are called to put down what the captains call 'a mutiny': the crew wouldn't work without a pay rise. Two Chinese crewmen are shot dead. An inquest finds that each of the Australian soldiers who fired the lethal shots 'acted in the course of his duty'. Soon after that, ten Dutch ratings are sent aboard the Dutch tanker *Sareona*, with rifles and fixed bayonets and instructions to round up Chinese crew members who are involved in another pay dispute. The Perth *Daily News* reports: 'One of the crew fell behind the rest so he was bayoneted.' Just like that. The rest of the crew panics and four Chinese are shot, one fatally.

The US submarine flotilla also starts arriving in March 1942. Over the next three years more than 170 submarines, mostly American, are based along North Wharf, along with their mother ships. The impact on Fremantle is great. More than two hundred civilians work at the base repairing damage from depth charges, some of friendly origin. Supplying the submarines is a formidable task as each vessel leaves on marathon six-week missions. There are also some unofficial suppliers. Walter Temby drives through the North Wharf checkpoint one evening. The guard orders him to stop. Instead Temby accelerates and is shot dead. In the car are 41 bottles of

British submarines, looking evil,
Fremantle, c1943.
[Saxon Fogarty]

beer, apparently intended for the US submariners — at inflated prices. The driver pays the highest price.

The Perth *Mirror* is a mildly titillating paper which prospers with stories suggesting that the submariners, like other American servicemen, prey not only on Japanese oil tankers but also on local women. The *Mirror* tells its readers of a fanciful evening at the port:

> *They* [Fremantle women] *swept across the port as the sun went down and joined sailors in orgies in ships, landing barges, cargo sheds and under the wharf itself. An Allied serviceman* [code for American] *is bewildered. 'They never ask for money. They don't want cigarettes. I can only think they must be sex maniacs.'*

The *Mirror* story is based on a single fact. Two women are gaoled for being idle and disorderly in Fremantle. Idle? Unlikely. Mabel Troy responds to the *Mirror*'s claim. These can't be Fremantle women, who are too busy working and cooking, and doing the house to have time for uninhibited partying on Victoria Quay.

The port of Fremantle sees more than preparations for war: it later sees war's results, with waves of post-war migrants. But before that others were drawn to an earlier Fremantle by local

A meeting place under Victoria Quay?
[Martin Webster]

Child migrants arrive on the Asturius, *1947. Some 'orphans' turned out to have parents.*
[Saxon Fogarty]

events. Nineteen thousand, mostly gold seekers, arrived in 1895 at the Long Jetty. At other times there were Chinese farmhands, some of whom irrigate vegetables using wooden buckets, along the fertile river flats in North Fremantle, while others work in laundries in Market Street. Later there are a limited number of Irish convicts, labourers and pub keepers, and British 'agricultural workers' who may never have worked on a farm before they are dropped off, ill-equipped and helpless, among the karri in the south-west. In the 1920s Russians escaping civil war arrive.

Displaced Europeans come first after the Second World War, in sketchily engineered American Liberty ships. Australia's colour-conscious Minister for Immigration, Arthur Calwell, is at Fremantle to welcome the 100,000th of them: 'You are obviously the right type. I notice many of you are tall and fair.' Much earlier the arrival of the wrong type, Chinese and Japanese migrants, stops with Federation and the introduction of the White Australia Policy. This means a Japanese brothel in Bannister Street opposite the Palms grinds to a halt for want of new staff. But how does the brothel in High Street that caters for Japanese naval officers regularly bring in new staff? Street talk says it's part of a plan to keep our Japanese allies happy. And what better way …?

In the 1950s there are Portuguese arriving, thousands of

Friendly visit, 1935: Japanese warship loads with coal from a Fremantle hulk.
[A Orloff]

southern Italians, and many thousands of Ten Pound Poms and others under the Bring Out a Briton scheme. Survivors of the Hungarian revolution in 1956 start to arrive. Today Tony Jones' sculpture, beside a gangplank at E shed, captures in bronze an anxious new arrival. He is greeted by a dingo. The dingo is often the first image of Australia the 'foreigners' have seen from their ships, painted in red on Dingo Flour Mills in North Fremantle (some say by an apprentice sign-writer and migrant named Alan Bond but they are probably wrong). The dingo, like many other locals, seems apprehensive about the European. The apprehension is mutual — and shared by Fremantle dogs who snarl as they pass.

Unlike the Eastern Europeans, the thousands of southern Italians are stocky and dark. Nunzio Gumina, Sicilian, six and skinny, is one of the newcomers. Nunzio's will become perhaps the best known face in the Fremantle of the 1980s but this day in February, 1954, he is standing at the rail of a crowded migrant ship with his mother Lucia. They are scanning the wharf for Pietro, their father and husband. They haven't seen him for two years. He was a member of the carabinieri at Capo d'Orlando until he refused to bash a prisoner to get information. A peaceable policeman had poor prospects in Sicily at the time and he soon left for Fremantle with his eldest son.

Nunzio describes his first day at South Terrace Primary School (now Fremantle Primary School and situated in Alma Street) in *Wharf Rats*, the school's centenary publication:

> *On my first day, the school bell rang and I sat down to eat my lunch (half a loaf of bread stuffed with a crayfish) on the grass. A bigger boy came over to me and looked at my crayfish loaf. You're Italian. Biff. When I came to I was summoned by a group of Italian boys to the back of the toilet block.*

'Tomorrow you'll have to teach him a lesson,' he's told. And he does this by jumping on the big boy's back and hitting him on the nose with a roundhouse punch. The Italian kids cheer. Nunzio feels he has been selected for the team. But despite the number of nationalities present this is still a unicultural society. Nunzio improves his prospects with members of the dominant team by swapping his salami or crayfish sandwiches for 'more normal' Australian Vegemite delights. Fifty years later Nunzio tells me how Lucia cooks crayfish in her copper in the back yard of 8 Howard Street. I express surprise at such luxury: Nunzio chides me. 'Crayfish was our food not a luxury.' He calls Fremantle of the fifties Crayfish City. It could never be Rock Lobster City.

In the late fifties someone decides Fremantle should put on

Nick Rotondella and Sam Paino,
58 Market Street, 1964.
[Fremantle City Library: Local History Collection]

Busy day at the passenger terminal, c1965.
[Fremantle Ports]

a more welcoming face for the newcomers, rather than lining them up with their baggage in a bare cargo shed to await customs clearance. We construct a classy passenger terminal after demolishing two old cargo sheds. Politicians say 'It's unique; unique in the world in fact.' Two hundred metres long, it's a structure worthy of tautology. The joinery and finish are said to be like a good 1960s city hotel. Not too many know what that's like but perhaps the newcomers will now be more enthusiastic when asked 'What do you think of Western Australia?' as they step from their ship. They don't arrive by ship for much longer.

Passenger jets start arriving as the terminal opens and the passenger liners stop. Labour-saving techniques are introduced for cargo ships,and their impact on the bustle of commercial activity up and down High Street is still felt. A leftover from the early migration times is the Migration and Information Office of 1906 on Victoria Quay where A O Neville, later the controversial arbiter on race as Chief Protector of Aborigines, conscientiously passes out pamphlets to new arrivals extolling life in the Western Australian bush. The office is still virtually intact and accessible within the Old Police Station complex.

Fremantle's migrant culture adds several strata in the 1970s and 1980s with the arrival by jet of escapees from oppression in South America, particularly Chile. They bring drums with them and drumming becomes a major Fremantle sound again. Drums are not new at the port. They attracted patrons and pugilists to fights with a few pennies thrown into the ring as purses in the Depression. These fights took place behind the Newcastle Club Hotel (now the Newport after a name change inspired by the America's Cup defence). The drums were beaten by boxing instructors who always seemed to be called 'Sailor' or 'Tiger'. Drums also drew patrons from the railway station to Uglyland, the fun fair run by the Ugly Men's Association, a service organisation, on what is now Pioneer Reserve. It can be very hard to hold a meeting in Fremantle without drummers somewhere providing a noisy backdrop.

The buildings of Fremantle's West End, like the port itself, tell rich stories to anyone who will listen. I'm strolling near 77 Pakenham Street, the Victoria Coffee Palace of 1895, then the Burlington Guest House and now the Backpackers Hotel. I bump into Bill Latter. He's a Fremantle celebrity: trade unionist, former Communist Party of Australia member, coal miner. A conservative premier, David Brand, calls the Collie Miners' Union the Latter Day Saints. Bill becomes Fremantle's deputy mayor. He is a wise man — with a touch of dogmatism — and a historian of the anti-German riots in Fremantle in 1915 and 1916, when 'German' comes to mean anyone who isn't British. Very often it means Greek.

Nikola Zaknich and Nikola Silich herring fishing off Rottnest, c1970.
[Hugh Schmitt; Western Australian Maritime Museum]

Bill tells me that during the First World War members of the Industrial Workers of the World (IWW, commonly known as the Wobblies) stayed at the Burlington. Government spooks believe the IWW is anti-war and generally subversive which, of course, it is. There are elaborate show trials and many Wobblies are deported. The spooks watch the postbox opposite No. 77. Letters posted by IWW members — and lots of others besides — are seized and read for evidence of sedition. You can't argue with Bill about spooks. He reads all the police spook files. In later times he has one of his own.

The Wobblies move to small farms, bordered by narrow lanes and mulberry and fig trees in White Gum Valley, behind the limestone ridge that frames Fremantle. Here they await the turmoil which will follow the 'inevitable' dismantling of capitalism after the Russian Revolution. If this doesn't happen they are certain to be excluded from the system. Either way they'll be short of a feed. So they grow their own. Each week they bring produce to Sarah Jane Edwards, widow of the working class martyr, who runs a small shop in Price Street, leased for her by the Fremantle Lumpers' Union. The image of Sarah Jane kneeling among the rubble to shelter her stricken husband from the sun makes her a saint among lumpers. Legend on the wharf is that she never remarried. This is not true.

White Gum Valley:
safe haven for the Wobblies, c1916.
[Fremantle City Library: Local History Collection]

On another afternoon, again outside No. 77, I meet John Troy, son of the revered union leader Paddy, and himself a former seaman, local GP and, briefly, state ALP member for Fremantle — briefly, because he is thought to be more interested in Arab than Fremantle issues. He sees them as being much the same. John's mother Mabel first meets Paddy here when, in 1926, he drops in for his ninepenny three-course meal while his ship, a Geraldton dredge, is being refitted in Fremantle. Mabel Nielson is the waitress at the Burlington boarding house run by her mother, serving ninepenny three-course meals. By 1929 there are many in Fremantle who don't have ninepence, but Alice Nielson always has food available. She is quickly sent bankrupt. The bailiff places a large padlock on the front door to secure her only equity, the furniture and bedding. That night her friends arrive with a ladder to retrieve the furniture through an upstairs window. Such retrievals are happening all over Fremantle. John takes me to the Fremantle Workers' Club, clad in beige wall tiles *circa* 1960, at 9 Henry Street. This is where Paddy Troy's membership application is blackballed. John tells me who blackballed him and why. It is a story that epitomises the gothic nature of Fremantle union politics and the fact that Paddy is a communist. Not everyone on the wharf likes a communist. Coherence among lumpers can be exaggerated, labour historian Stuart Macintyre observes.

Alice Nielson, manager of the Burlington, and her grandson, John Troy, ready to go to his first 'demo', 1947.
[Hazel Butorac]

Peter Schipperheyn, the 'Michelangelo of Melbourne', with his Stations of the Cross, 1996.
[Michael Wearne]

Following page: Wool heads majestically for the port from Elder's Pakenham Street woolstore, 1928.
[Stuart Gore; The Battye Library — BA352/5]

While strolling in Pakenham Street south of High Street, try looking for short cuts to get you back to Arthur Head. Peer through lanes and doorways. It's surprising what you'll find An 1860s cottage perhaps, or an old wall — or a locked gate. Start at No. 31, the 1860 Dalgety's warehouse, built when the streets running between the ocean and river jetties were becoming important and where drays drawn by muscular Clydesdales deliver wool. Walk through to Henry Street along an avenue bordered by modern studio units. The vast roof has been removed. Next move through the old Bateman complex, now the courtyard of the University of Notre Dame (UND). Follow the Stations of the Cross attached to the walls. The stations may be central to the Catholic ritual but are frequently bad art. The stylised bronze reliefs by Melbourne artist Peter Schipperheyn are stunning exceptions. And for anyone interested in symbols the UND chapel has as its altar a carpenter's workbench, discovered during restoration work.

Now imagine the southern end of Henry Street in the late 1960s. The elaborately detailed warehouses look increasingly neglected; roofs with nails missing flap in the wind inviting decay and then destruction. Gordon Stephenson, who had been an associate in Paris of the celebrated Swiss architect of the 'engineering design' and town planner, Le Corbusier, came to Fremantle in 1955 when preparing a plan for the future of

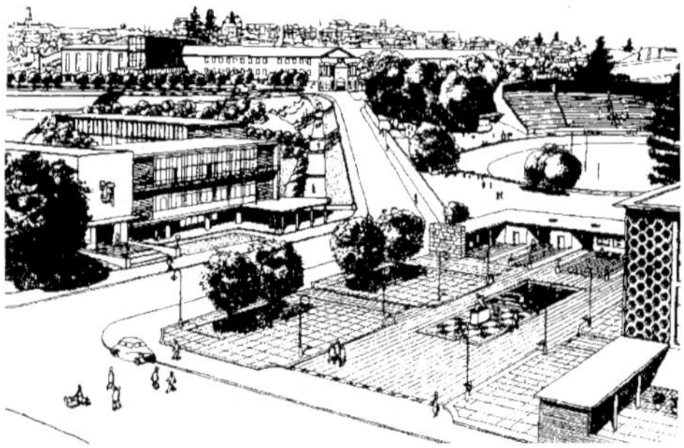

Metropolitan Regional Plan for how Fremantle's east side might look, in the 1950s (top); and the east end of High Street before a development spree and the mall.
[Fremantle City Library: Local History Collection]

Perth and its regions. He wanted to allow the free movement of many cars and to accommodate large numbers of manual workers, who never arrived. He also admired Fremantle's West End and wanted to keep it intact. His plan included a coastal highway to be built around Fremantle's gold rush buildings. By the sixties this had become plans for a highway through Henry Street. The Orient Hotel is waiting to be pulled down to make way for a boat showroom for controversial builder Len Buckeridge. High Street will also be widened by removing the elaborate facades along both sides of the street.

Then attitudes change in the 1970s and the highway plans are scrapped. But planning blight is another threat. With the future of the buildings uncertain no-one will spend money on them: they become derelict and seem likely to be lost anyhow. Eventually, the buildings and their histories are saved by a Hawke government America's Cup grant for their restoration. The Dawkins brothers — John, the local federal member of parliament and Commonwealth finance minister, and Jeremy, the city's Director of Planning — prove to be a fruitful combination for Fremantle.

Study of the Moores Building in Henry Street reveals a rich Fremantle story. With construction booming in 1899, a facade is wrapped around the various buildings on the site including the town house, the result of thirty-six years of business

Behind its classical, all enveloping facade, the Moores Building is a collection of structures, passages and openings, 1988.

[Brent Sumner; Fremantle City Library: Local History Collection]

development by the general merchant, William Dalgety Moore. He warehouses and retails, roasts coffee, grinds pepper, blends tea, offers a mail order service, exports pearl shell to Paris button makers, and imports 'Chinese coolies'. He has a reputation for fairness but can be a hard man. In 1881 a Chinese indentured labourer dies on his way to the Shark Bay pearling grounds. Moore refuses to pick up the tab for his burial: the labourer represents 'faulty goods'. The government ends up paying. (Moore and his first and second wives produced a total of nineteen children. It's appropriate that Woodside, his mansion in East Fremantle, later becomes a busy maternity hospital — recently closed.)

A three-level store at the rear of the Moore's complex was built earlier to hold meat slaughtered on the site. The meat goes to the adjoining factory and emerges as canned mutton. The store is a refined little building performing a prosaic task. Its shingle roof can be seen from the small parking area on the west side of Pakenham Street. The black stones dotting the limestone walls must have come out as ship's ballast. If you don't find your way from Henry to Mouat Street use Croke Street, which takes you through the old Bateman Hardware properties where, in its heyday, to ask for a stick of solder meant being shown up to six different combinations of lead and tin. It was that sort of hardware store. Eventually you are back in Cliff Street.

Cliff Street in 1900 is still the street of those historian Patricia Brown calls the 'Merchant Princes'. They have been using their own vessels to ship cattle and sheep to Fremantle from their extensive properties in the north, gathering pearl shell for Paris button makers and making a fortune selling hardware and furniture and women's clothing while financing elaborate gold rush buildings. You'll find the office of one of the state's richest men and one of colonial journalist Andree Hayward's ironic list of the 'seven hungry families', George Shenton, at No. 41. Imagine a large brass plate to the right of his doorway promoting Nobel Explosives, one of his agencies. On a windy day the waves from the river and ocean still wash the street of the Merchant Princes.

In 1900 the merchant James Lilly, dubbed the Father of Western Australian Shipping, builds the handsome structure across the road from Shenton at No. 38, which still carries Lilly's name. Here he dreams of bigger ponds and laments his lack of interaction with the rest of the world even though his ships carry sandalwood to as far away as China. It's said he's addicted to alcohol and other drugs. He is said to be a 'citizen of the old school' but his occasional violent outbursts cause residents to mutter about 'syphilitic dementia'. In 1905 Lilly takes the train to Claremont, buys strychnine from a chemist

Bateman's hardware in the 1970s: six sorts of solder.
[Michal Lewi]

explaining that he wants to poison a dog, and consumes it in a vacant block. He dies in the 'greatest agony'. NO DRUGS OR MONEY KEPT ON THESE PREMISES says a notice placed in one of the windows, posted by the current occupant, 'Painless Pat', a dentist. Well, it did say that but on my last visit the notice had gone. Eighty years after the merchant's death, a towering youth throws baskets at the back of the Lilly Building. He is Lucan Longley, later of the Chicago Bulls, the US National Basketball Association's champion team. His father Richard, architect and basketballer, has erected the ring, using a mock-up of a housing development as the backboard.

Walk down Croke Lane from Cliff Street. There's a small lane running to the right between the old flour mill and offices (No. 2) and a Dalgety warehouse. You'll see a stone warehouse with brick quoins. It is one of the early stores scattered around Cliff Street but it becomes famous in the 1980s as Timothy's Toys. Timothy — Gordon Kay — is the toy-maker from Central Casting and Timothy is his son. Gordon is a mild man from New Zealand who has worked in a bank and started here by making wooden toys for Tim. Gordon moves lovingly among his wooden toys which — perhaps *who* is a better word — have a deep lustrous finish after much sanding and repeated coats of lacquer. Clown mobiles propel themselves across the vast jarrah beams which are almost black from the fusion of age

Venice comes to Fremantle:
Cliff Street, 1926.
[A Orloff]

Following page: Gordon Kay, alias
Timothy the Toymaker.
[Fremantle City Library: Local History Collection]

and the salty atmosphere. There are rocking horses being restored and a relic of a wooden boat in which kids play. The toys are too good for children say some parents — and too expensive — but Gordon's toys become a target for those same parents, and for America's Cup tourists. Then he dies of cancer leaving Arthur Head sad — particularly its toys. The store becomes a carpenter's workshop.

Walk on to Whalers Tunnel, which is safe again after some creative engineering consolidates its roof and stops it from shedding large slabs of limestone. The tunnel was completed in January 1838 to link Whalers Jetty with Cliff and High Streets and avoid a long trip around encircling cliffs of a similar height to the Round House and sandhills. In 1838 whaling is the colony's one flourishing industry and operates largely from Bathers Beach. John Bateman's Fremantle Whaling Company on the south side of the river mouth competes with Josh Harwood's Perth Fishing Company on the north, pursuing a variety of whales passing between the mainland and Rottnest on their spring migration. The sperm whale with its 20 tons of oil is rare and becoming rarer — its predictable appearances make it an easy target for men waiting with harpoons. The Bateman side of the industry had a jetty, a breakwater, station house, and a substantial cave used as the whalers' store. Whaler and other ships are built at the Mews boatyard just north of the

Mews boatyard and the derelict Bateman whale fishery beneath the Arthur Head bluff, c1890.
[Fremantle City Library: Local History Collection]

tunnel entrance, between 1837 and 1860. The foundations of the boatyard and the tryworks where the oil was extracted were revealed in an exploratory dig in the 1990s then buried again to conserve the delicate ruins until they can be safely displayed. The Whalers Jetty sea wall is clearly visible.

Whales at the time of the Bateman fishery have little protection. David Blutchart recalls 'watching the fun' from high ground when he was a boy in the 1840s: 'Sometimes they would chase a big fellow all day without tiring him out. When they made fast with a harpoon the whale would go like mad. You couldn't see the boat for foam and when the whale came up to blow, two great fans of water would shoot out.' This is a dangerous game. Sometimes a Bateman boat would be attacking a whale from one side and a Harwood boat from the other. Only in falling darkness will the crews cut a whale free. The oil is too valuable. The American whalers agree to avoid the Fremantle area but are better equipped and can hunt up and down the coast.

The tunnel encapsulates several layers of history which would have pleased Henry Reveley its designer; he wanted it to have a life or two after whaling, which he thought could not be sustained. Such new uses may coalesce with uses of the Round House immediately above. A police sergeant with a family of twelve lives in the Round House just before the First World

View from the Whalers Tunnel looking west to Bathers Beach, 1892.
[West Australian Newspapers]

View from the Whalers Tunnel looking east up High Street, c1900.
[Fremantle City Library: Local History Collection]

War and keeps pigs and chooks in the tunnel. Fishermen use it as a smoker for local mackerel, herring and mullet. It even contains the exit from the Secret Tunnel which runs down from the cliff top to allow soldiers, maritime pilots and gunners and their families to escape from exposed gun emplacements and shelter from the air attacks which seem inevitable in 1942. Kathleen Wilson, the lighthouse keeper's daughter who grew up in the 1920s in a semi-detached dwelling near the Round House, reports that Whalers Tunnel was taboo for the kids living nearby. Their parents said it was an evil and dangerous place which meant the kids often went there to frighten themselves with the eerie echoes of their own voices. In the 1970s well-worn men in well-worn overcoats arrive at the tunnel each evening: they and their devoted dogs curl into any crevice to avoid the westerlies and salty spray. While you're there check the rock itself. It is a beautiful piece of sculpting by wind, etching by water-borne chemicals and quarrying by humans — often on a chain gang.

With whaling on the wane the colony stagnates in the 1840s. Whales have been overfished by the Americans and kerosene is replacing whale oil as a source for lighting in homes. Whalebone (actually whalefin) is still used by corset makers, dressmakers and milliners, although it is expensive.

Only 416 people live in Fremantle in 1840. William

Power arrives for the trams, 1905.
[Fremantle Society Collection]

Start of a dynasty:
the Samson family, 1858.
[Fremantle City Library: Local History Collection]

Samson goes to the new colony in South Australia while Lionel leaves for England to pursue the well-connected, and much younger, Frances (Fanny) Levi. They return married in 1843 and for the next ten years Fanny is the only Jewish woman in Western Australia. Lionel and Fanny start the Samson dynasty with six children, two of them becoming mayors of Fremantle. The family lives in Fanny's Cottage which still stands south of the Samson company offices in Cliff Street.

Lionel Samson worries, as do other merchants, about the colony's shortage of labour and capital, particularly in Fremantle. They want convicts to boost the labour force and believe their introduction will bring with it British government capital to allow stores, bridges, roads and a prison to be built. Lionel, the family man, also worries that this fragile outpost of Empire could be overrun by wild men with a single stolen cannon and writes to the Governor. But the debate is cut short. The British response is positive and so rapid that the *Scindian* arrives in June 1850 with seventy-five convicts and fifty guards, ahead of the ship which carries the declaration that convictism in Western Australia is approved. There have been no preparations. Use of Whalers Tunnel has slowed and it is suggested as a temporary dormitory for the convicts: just install some straw mattresses. The efficiency advocates say this will save ten minutes per convict per day in getting to work at the government stores being built in Cliff Street and improving the makeshift — and dangerous — outer harbour. It's decided to hold the newcomers in a modified and extended version of Captain Daniel Scott's warehouse on Marine Terrace while waiting until they build their permanent home, the Convict Establishment, which increasingly dominates the city from Church Hill. In 1866 Royal Engineers direct parties of convict labourers to build the first bridge across the Swan. It is severely humped so that lighters can pass underneath on their way to the capital which the locals think should not be the capital at all, particularly following the surge of convict-built infrastructure in Fremantle. Part of the rich legend of the escape artist Moondyne Joe is that he crosses the bridge first, after one of his many break-outs from the Convict Establishment. Moondyne wouldn't get the joke but, with the sons of Fremantle merchants still being educated in classics in British private schools, the first bridge was frequently referred to as the Bridge of Styx.

Until the end of colonial rule in 1890, governors spend time in Fremantle. The Convict Establishment creates a number of embarrassing problems: yet another escape by Moondyne Joe or the fiasco which sees six Fenian prisoners walk through the gates and sail away on the American whaler, *Catalpa.*

There are consolations like the Residency, a comfortable

Railway Bridge, c1895.
[Beatel and Williams]

Last train to Fremantle,
Christmas Eve, 2004.
[Sophie Van Der Leeden]

Shenton stables (left), the Residency (large single-storey building, centre) and the first lighthouse (right), Arthur Head, c1870.
[The Battye Library — 816B/TB/249]

house with a sea breeze in summer (and gales in winter), just north of Arthur Head. One governor with problems at the Convict Establishment is William Robinson. I think of him while parking my car in the car park which, until the 1950s, was the site of the Residency. Governor Robinson was a popular colonial administrator with a patrician profile and considerable musical skills. He puts the bombastic *Ode to Western Australia* to music and children insist on singing it to him wherever he goes. Despite this he generally likes Western Australia. He is an observer of life around High and Cliff Streets and is not impressed with Fremantle which he dismisses in 1873 as a 'mere seaport lockup for drunken sailors and prostitutes'. He might have added for off-season pearlers and the shadowy demimonde of ticket-of-leave men and their turbulent children who live around Captain Scott's original convict quarters on South Bay. It does time as an asylum and ends up as the site of the extended Esplanade Hotel.

I pass the building site early one morning while out walking in 1983. A striking woman, dressed in orange, is painting on a corrugated iron gate: THE PRICE OF BLISS IS RUBBER GLOVES. I ask her what that means and she says it has 'something to do with AIDS', which is just becoming a concern, with various 'protective' measures being put forward.

The pearlers who embellish Governor Robinson's description of Fremantle arrive in the 'city of public houses' from Broome and Shark Bay with plenty of cash at the end of a dangerous season. Historian Patricia Brown notes sex is one of 'Fremantle's maritime service industries'. Close to the harbour area is a supply of brothels with an international flavour — French, English, Italian but predominantly Japanese whose staff are 'kimono clad and dignified' and even pretend they are about other things like running a laundry.

Xavier Herbert is a pharmacist, wild boy and wild man, and author. He provides a graphic picture of his Fremantle in *Disturbing Element*, an autobiography with a substantial dose of fiction. He lived in Fremantle in the 1910s and twenties but his Fremantle probably starts at the time of Governor Robinson and extends for fifty years:

> *Fremantle is no less colourful than its waterfront, peopled as it largely was by seafarers and globetrotters that the ships of half a century had left behind. The packed shops and restaurants, wine bars, pubs, hash-houses, wash-houses, whore-houses, doss-houses, were run by people of all breeds.*
>
> *Most famous of the moll-shops was Lopey's, run by a little old Welshwoman espoused to an ancient cut-throat from Cuba, Lopez. Two other defenders of molls were an Irishman*

Master pearler, Captain Frank Biddles and wife, Blanche, 'out for a spin in Singapore', 1909.
[Fremantle City Library: Local History Collection]

named Dublin Dan and a Negro, Dixie Plum, giants of men and terrible rivals who frequently slugged it out …

Of nights the bars fumed and roared, the drunks bawled and brawled and wept and puiked [sic], *the Salvos and the Brethren banged their drums and pumped their organs and ranted of the wrath to come, the picture shows and vaudevilles rocked to the excitement of the patrons, and Tiptoe Alley resounded with shrieks, giggles, guffaws, and the bellowing of those champions Dublin Dan and Dixie Plum.*

Xavier Herbert's text comes from memory many years later and almost certainly from his imagination. Social historian Raelene Davidson relies on police notebooks and magistrates' records. She reports that streetworkers were an important element of the port streetscape. Clad in chemisettes, with bare arms, bright stockings and boldly painted faces, they are highly visible and solicit sailors and port workers from shop doorways and verandahs or leaning over front gates. Such must have been the modus operandi, if not the dress description, of Mary Ann Coates (later Collins) gaoled in 1897 for vagrancy — that is, two convictions for soliciting. Later, she is running a refined house at No. 48 Essex Street, called Rose Cottage, then Mary Ann's (also known as The Palms) at No. 9 Bannister Street. Income from The Palms and timely real estate purchases in

Fire at the Nairn Street flour mill, 1901. Xavier Herbert noted: 'Fremantle onlookers at fires were enthralled by the never-failing rumour that someone was trapped inside.'
[Fremantle City Library: Local History Collection]

Market Street in the foreground, and Bannister Street at right angles to it, running to the waterfront, c1890. South Jetty (left) and Long Jetty are in the distance.
[Royal Western Australian Historical Society]

Perth's Roe Street mean she is probably Fremantle's richest woman when she dies in North Fremantle in 1939.

Mary Ann is small and businesslike and drifts easily up Bannister Street and into the turn-of-the-century shoppers crowding High Street and South Terrace. Madame Marie Guidotti, Mrs Collins' rival working from a Suffolk Street establishment, displays no such reticence. She promenades in her tasteful black dress twirling a parasol from Paris. Two black poodles on black leads complete the picture.

Brian Klopper is a Fremantle architect whose buildings have a quite distinctive look. Any property built with recycled bricks comes to be called in the real estate pages 'Klopper Inspired'. Klopper likes to do some physical work with bricks, timber and iron on the construction site. This day he is working on a number of shops and apartments in Bannister Street, opposite the Fremantle Club. A weather-beaten old worker stops to watch — and talk. 'What are you going to call the shops,' he wants to know. Klopper says they might be The Pines, explaining there are two Norfolk pines out the back and there was a brothel of that name nearby. The old man splutters. 'It was The Palms not The Pines. It was on the other side of the road, down near the corner with Pakenham Street. It cost five bob a rut.' Then he moves on to supervise another construction site.

It should be said that for Fremantle, pearling means more

than just wealth for the merchants and seasonal carousing for the crews. Jewellers — including a family firm named Pearl in High Street — expertly skin and set the pearls. The building of luggers booms around Arthur Head and Alfred Brown's shipyard on Marine Terrace turns out two hundred. These are about eleven metres long and particularly fast. Pearling also leads to the South Jetty being extended to 139 metres. Then Long Jetty is built and frequently extended: finally, at two kilometres, with its double railway line, it is indeed a long jetty and doglegs from Anglesea Point into deep water. When the new inner harbour opens in 1897 Long Jetty becomes a promenade for men in blazers and straw boaters and women in long dresses and large hats. A few piles are still visible south of Arthur Head.

The times and the distance between ports bring a share of well-groomed pirates and con artists to Fremantle where they meet colonial governors and local financiers on High Street. Bully Hayes who arrives in 1857 with an unpaid-for cargo from Singapore is both buccaneer and trickster. He moves speedily ahead of his reputation which is, according to historian J K Hitchcock, that of 'pirate, searover, blackbirder and debaucher of white and coloured women and children'. The hard-heads of Fremantle maritime commerce along Cliff and High Streets are readily taken in by this handsome,

Alfred Brown's boatyard, c1900.
[Fremantle City Library: Local History Collection]

Carpenter Bill Leonard working with an adze on the Duyfken *replica, 1997.*
[Michael Wearne]

HS.

Long Jetty, c1896. Check the hat and boot appearing from the cargo basket.
[Beatel and Williams]

Previous page: A speedy pearling lugger, one of hundreds from Alfred Brown's boatyard, heads for Broome, c1900.
[Fremantle Society Collection]

stylishly dressed young man who dances and sings well. Soon he is engaged to the daughter of harbourmaster Daniel Scott, although apparently not to be married. He moves on and is called 'Fremantle's last buccaneer' after he is murdered by a crewman. The America's Cup celebrations — then deflations — put the lie to this description.

Next con artist to tie up at South Jetty is Fremantle's 'prince of romancers' — the voluble Louis de Rougemont, who arrives with a superior provenance. As Louis Grin he's been valet to Governor Robison. He cons High Street's maritime and commercial identities Owston, Pearse and McCleery into funding him on a pearling venture in the state's north-west. They are never repaid. Then he cons himself a cutter, the *Ada*, and a cargo, and eventually reaches England where he writes a series of stories in *Wide World* magazine, supposedly based on his exploits, but actually created from books in the British Library.

High Street is getting specialist shops and services as Fremantle becomes important. In 1863 Daniel Congdon sets up as a dispenser and compounder of medicines. His father is a pharmacist at the Convict Establishment and young Daniel readily picks up enough knowledge to start his own business. He sells Weston's Wizard Oil which, when swallowed or massaged externally, relieves 'nervous diseases and inflammatory aches and pains, curing rheumatism, sciatica, gout, neuralgia, cholera, coughs and colds, scrofula, piles ...' He also sells 'every article of attire requisite Ladies' summer and winter wear'. This line proves more profitable and, when other chemists arrive in town, Daniel Congdon concentrates on Ladies' Wear. Congdon becomes the first of a number of pharmacists to be elected Mayor of Fremantle.

The merchants' dominance ebbs from the 1880s but their names and influence linger on. This is not surprising as the merchants are extremely prolific. Organised labour and smaller industrial businesses gradually become the new powers in Fremantle. Industry replaces commerce as the major employer, particularly of women. Mills and Ware the biscuit makers, Allens the cool drink manufacturers, and other food processors move into town — sometimes starting in tin sheds. There is also Pearse Brothers, makers of boots and shoes in North Fremantle, and WA Brushware, a big employer in East Fremantle. As a consequence working-class women's activism develops. The tailoresses have a union by 1896 and the women at Pearse Brothers uppers section have their first strike over wages in 1916, although it lasts only one minute. George Pearse says to Clara Crowther and other workers: 'Take your hat and coat and go home.' Strike ends.

The remarkable Jean Beadle moves to Fremantle from the

Quiet flows the Swan, past
North Fremantle, 1923.
[A Orloff]

Demure dancing at the Sailors' Rest, c1942.
[Saxon Fogarty]

Victorian goldfields where she had been a founding member of the Labor Women's Organisation. She establishes Western Australia's Women's Political and Social Crusade after a lively meeting at Fremantle in 1905. Later the Social Crusade becomes the Women's Labor League which states that even if a woman is working forty hours a week she should also have the skills for housework. The pioneer feminist movement, the Women's Christian Temperance Movement, arrives in Fremantle in 1892 with a political and social agenda which goes way beyond attacks on alcohol and the establishing of coffee palaces. They advocate women's suffrage but in Fremantle they also take up a particular local issue. 'Every sailor needs a mother in every port,' they say and set about furnishing rented rooms for seamen in the Masonic Hall while building the Sailors' Rest next door in Marine Terrace as a place where sailors can rest between ships and after shipwrecks which still occur off Fremantle. This is a decidedly middle class organisation with respected Fremantle names like Mrs Bateman and Mrs Pearse and Mrs Captain Smith listed among 'the hardest workers'. Around town doubts are expressed whether such women should be associating with sailors.

The state's economic activity moves from gold to golden grain and wool. The increasing production is railed, stored, processed, packed and dispatched to and from the streets crossing High Street — Cliff, Mouat and Henry. The lumpers, who will reach a membership peak of 2500 after the Second World War, work at a number of stages in the process. They form an association in 1889, with the egalitarian Merchant Prince Arthur Diamond as president and the hot-tempered Harry Marshall as founding secretary. The lumpers are an assertive lot. When the West Australian Steamship Owners post a notice at the entrance to the wharf in February 1899 announcing lowering wages and clearly designed to crush the Lumpers' Union, there is an immediate strike. Shipping managers are jeered when they appear in High and Phillimore Streets near the harbour, and violence breaks out when an attempt is made to employ non-union workers. For five weeks the struggle continues. It takes the appointment of an unusual arbitrating team of Anglican Bishop C O L Riley, Catholic Bishop Matthew Gibney (who's had experience as a negotiator with the Kelly Gang at Glenrowan) and the Reverend George E Rowe, chair of the Methodist Church Congress, to negotiate a solution. It was Fremantle's first glimpse of industrial arbitration.

This solidarity of the lumpers is shown in a number of their rituals. One wharfside practice starts at the Lionel Samson bottling plant under their main office and involves pouring boiling water into empty whisky casks waiting to be shipped to

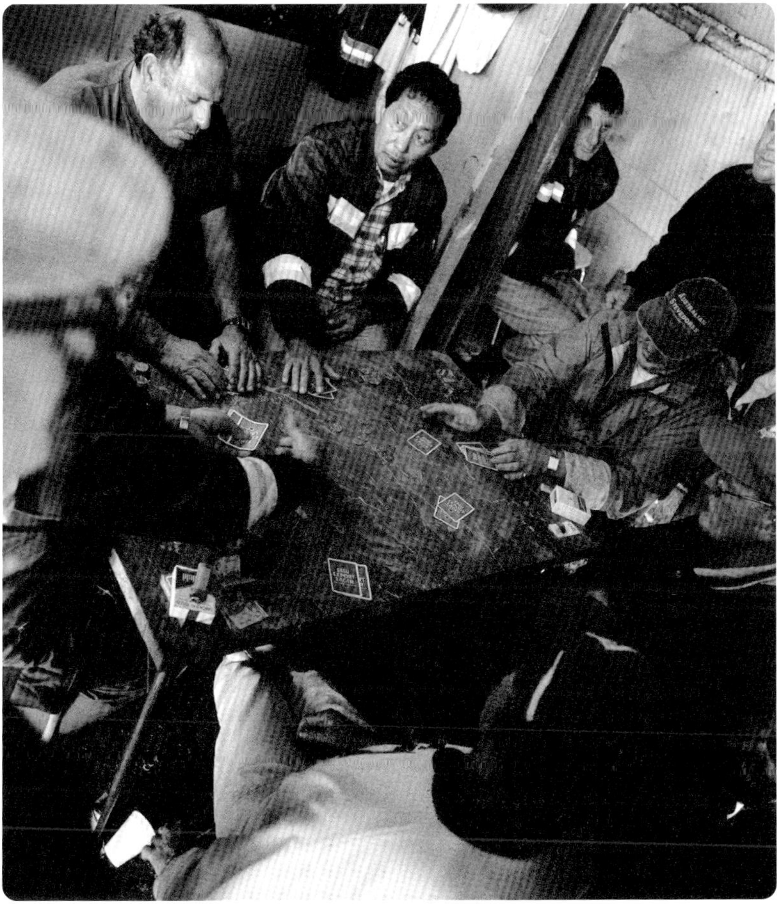

Card players during the
Patrick's wharf dispute, 1998.
[Daniel Bruyn]

distillers. The water is vigorously swirled around the cask: out comes a warming, well-oaked, whisky-infused drink that counteracts the cold. The lumpers call it Swirl and drink it from their big billies. Then there's the ritual of the annual Lumpers' Picnic, often held at the South Perth Zoo, when every lumper gets out his best suit and most Fremantle kids become lumpers' children for the day. Mothers with infants line their prams along the East Street jetty. It is Jim Dix's job in the 1930s, as the youngest lumper, to transport the prams to South Perth's Mends Street Jetty in a truck borrowed from one of the shipping companies, and to have them waiting, in the same order, when the steamer *Zephyr* arrives.

In the Fremantle Cemetery in High Street the final ritual of the Fremantle Lumpers' Union is played out. The union buries its dead. Being a lumper is a dangerous business. It is not easy to shuffle along a plank with a 90 kilogram bag of wheat on your back: it is very easy to fall into a ship's hold or be hit by falling cargo, particularly timber. The sulphur and other dusts collecting on the workers' lungs kill more slowly, particularly when combined with the tar from self-rolled cigarettes. There's row upon row of lumpers' graves and those of their families at Fremantle Cemetery. Twelve hundred plots, all of similar design. The urn mounted on a marble column commemorating Tom Edwards, Working Class

On the way to the
Lumpers' Picnic, c1948.
[Saxon Fogarty]

The Lumpers Union buries its dead: a zoom lens view of their patch at Fremantle Cemetery, and Tom Edwards' final resting place, 2003.
[Michal Lewi]

Martyr, looks over the rest. All men are equal …

Death is not far removed from humour on the wharf. Kathleen Wilson writes of a lumper being knocked over the side of a ship he is unloading. Several days after the accident his body has still not surfaced. A foreman stevedore observes grumpily: 'He'll turn up. They all turn up on pay day.'

I am outside Watson's butcher shop at 71 High Street. It is closed, the paint is looking worn and the verandah has iron loose. I think how Fremantle through the twenties, thirties and forties is a cohesive town (except when the Fremantle football derby is played). The lumpers support local businesses: when there is a strike the businesses are expected to reciprocate. William 'Old Bill' Watson — Fremantle's conservative Independent federal member and the candidate John Curtin could never beat — brings around boxes of Watsonia bacon and sausages to the strike headquarters at Fremantle Trades Hall. The Watsonia shop at 71 High Street was a magic place: over thirty years the butchers never age. They sell every part of the pig — including dozens of sows' ears. On Saturday mornings Chinese restaurateurs pack the shop to purchase some surprising parts. I am there to buy one of the pieces of roasting pork which cram the street window. Then in 2004 the owner, an international food giant, closes its doors for the last time. I go down before five to watch the final chop but they close early. The last butcher in central Fremantle has gone — and the last unprepared-food shop in High Street.

After the wharfies, the woolies are the biggest union group in Fremantle. There are 1500 woolies in the 1950s, members of the more conservative Shop Assistants Union. They clean and pack the clip stored in warehouses in the short streets running north–south across High Street and in the cavernous stores in Cantonment Street. How do you tell a wharfie from a woolie? Women tell me the woolies have soft hands. It's the lanolin in the wool which ensures the soft touch. One day in High Street I meet Larry Foley, once a woolie and now an art dealer. Fremantle is funny like that. He has been talking at Gino's with J J Miller, who rode the Melbourne Cup winner Galilee in the 1960s and is one of the assertive and extensive Duggan–Miller–Regan–Neesham clan. JJ sits at Gino's and gives Larry a critique of the Sydney primitive painter Robert Dickerson who paints horses and jockeys and sad-eyed Depression kids. Then one morning Dickerson arrives from Sydney on a painting expedition. JJ takes him south to see a remnant of Fremantle's horse country. Days later all three swim at Port Beach, a reasonably well kept Fremantle secret. Dickerson looks across at the tanks and pipes and industrial depots scattered among the North Fremantle dunes. 'This is

A temporary resting place — quiet day at a Fremantle woolstore.
[Daniel Bruyn]

Four generations of the Miller–Duggan clan gather in 1913. The father of famous Western Australian horse-racing identity J J Miller, also John, is to the left of the dog.
[Larry Foley]

Jeffrey Smart country,' he remarks to JJ, who gets the joke.

One warm afternoon while walking in High Street Larry tells me that in the 1930s he could find his way around Fremantle with his eyes shut — just by following his nose. There's a spicy scent from the large stacks of freshly cut sandalwood and the special pong of sheep hides drying with an astringent backdrop of tanning bark along Beach and Russell Streets, and of rabbit skins in Essex Street, on their way to becoming hats and coats in the United States. There is also the slightly queasy smell of leather tanning in Russell Street and the robust smell of wool scouring: dirt and dags. Larry takes me to Swan Wool Scourers in North Fremantle in 1997. They are famous for cleaning fine wool. I watch grimy, greasy wool moving through a Heath Robinson collection of tubs, rakes, lanolin collectors and heaters. Many an inventive person may have modified the plant. At the end of the line Maria Randazza thrusts her arms into the warmed, creamy-white, soft and light fibre, as she has been doing for forty years. I am given a go. It is like picking up warm snow. At noon the plant is turned off. It will never run again. The land beside the river is too expensive for industrial use. The barbecue which follows is sad.

There are other smells. Fremantle veterans tell me J and W Bateman's warehouse in Henry Street exudes the smell of vanilla being added to their ready-mix custards. This scent still survives sixty years later when the University of Notre Dame takes over the Bateman properties and retains some mixing and packaging machines as interpretation. Meanwhile, in the thirties, in another building off Henry Street, young Pearlie Smith tends a vat where equal quantities of olive oil and bulk brilliantine bubble like a witch's brew. It is marketed in salvaged bottles, under the name Natty's Hair Tonic. The flashy fragrance complements the glistening effect it has on sir's hair.

The smells of earlier Fremantle were not all that good. In the 1880s everything goes into the cesspits in back yards in High Street. These may be dug close to the private wells which provide drinking water and close to the butchers who hang their carcasses over the footpath. It is an invitation for an epidemic — and Fremantle doesn't have a public hospital until 1897 when nurses move into The Knowle, Colonel Henderson's elegant and extensive Georgian mansion, which is still Fremantle's best kept secret. Walk off Alma Street towards the Children's Ward and look right. There it is, virtually intact.

The inevitable plague arrives in 1900. Rats come down ships' hawsers to trigger an outbreak of bubonic fever. Seven people die. Fremantle is shocked. The portents are not good. There is talk of Black Death and fears that it will spread quickly. Bodies are given multiple wrappings before being weighted and dumped in deep water beyond Garden Island.

Pietro Porcelli's evocative peace memorial in North Fremantle; and the Weeties factory provides a special early-morning aroma, 1992.
[Michael Wearne]

Morning tea at Fremantle Hospital on a bad hair day, 1918.
[Dr G Leyland]

Col. Henderson's home, The Knowle, now hidden within the hospital complex, 2003.
[Michal Lewi]

The Fremantle Board of Health is constantly on guard against further outbreaks. Ships' hawsers are coated with wet tar and plague rats are caught like flies on flypaper. Lumpers are fumigated if they've been working on foreign cargoes.

Larry, my guide, stops at 50 High Street where his father had his name painted on the window in brown and gold lettering — *GEORGE FOLEY Tobacconist and Turf Commission Agent* — alias SP bookie. Few Fremantle dwellers own cars in the thirties but Fremantle SP bookies like George and Jock Laurie and Alex Maru do. Their cars make statements about the bookie's importance in this workers' town. Bookies support their community in much the way Kate Leigh, Sydney's Queen of the Underworld, does hers in Surry Hills, albeit with money from different sources. In Alex Maru's case he'll back with an 18-gallon keg any community function. The only proviso is that the band plays Old Man River twice during the evening.

George Foley's car is a black Buick Straight 8. He is known as a smart dresser and has a light silk suit ready for a change when needed in summer. However, George is killed in 1935 when the Straight 8 overturns on a bend. Larry's mother Muriel opens a shop at 60 High Street and sells home-made confectionery. (The flat above No. 60 becomes known in the 1980s as the anarchist Freedom Collective's Libertarian

Resource Centre.) Meanwhile, the Foley family moves in above No. 50, from their comfortable house in East Fremantle. The red neon sign opposite flashes UNION STORES, keeping the family awake at night and making a point about the pervasive influence of unions in the town. Union Stores, at the corner of High and Henry, was built in 1895 as part of the Bateman hardware conglomerate but by 1905 it is an ironmonger, grocer and universal provider. The unions and food producers are the new boys on the block. When we first look in the shop windows, No. 50 is a sex shop advertising 'games for playful people'. It is now a second-hand book shop. No. 48 is where Nick the Greek ran the Majestic Fruit Palace and made memorable penny ice-creams and creamy milkshakes. Other Greeks run restaurants, fish and chip shops and grocery shops in Market Street and South Terrace as well as High Street. When we first look, No. 48 is shared by a maker of mediaeval dresses and a body piercer whose window display includes an image of an ear pierced by an extremely large safety pin. When I next look an antique dealer has moved in. I also discover that, in the 1990s, the activities of Madam Lash in an upstairs room are a point of interest. There is, I'm told, still a hole in the ceiling where an earnest protector of High Street morals gathered evidence, hour upon hour. I saw Madam Lash on stage during a writer's festival. I think she shows little creativity

A 1923 storm has just pounded the Beaconsfield Hotel (now Moondyne Joe's), but that doesn't stop the local SP bookie from settling with his punters, while his 'cockatoos' watch for the police.
[A Orloff]

Watch out for the train! High Street, c1895, is a Georgian street of the verge of change.
[Beatel and Williams]

in her professional name but her biceps are well formed.

High Street looks much the same in the 1930s as it did immediately after the building and shopping boom thirty years earlier which converted a restrained Georgian village into an opulent industrial-commercial centre. By 1905 there are tram lines starting to head north, south and east: Fremantle can now expand beyond a restrictive triangle with water bordering on two sides and a limestone ridge on the third. Workers do not need to live close to their workplace any more.

Larry and I meet Alec Smith, Fremantle's champion storyteller, expert on Fremantle's many ghosts and collector of lead soldiers. We walk towards the Fremantle Hotel which Alec's parents managed and where Alec lived in the same room for thirty years and the same building for forty, since he was born in 1929. He tells me of the time when the hotel's fine dining room was converted to a service hospital, with the wall and windows along Cliff Street protected by sandbags from bomb blasts on the wharf which is only 200 metres away. The hospital never has a patient. I say little. It's hard to get a word in. Alec and Larry talk of running from the Princess Theatre in Leake Street (now an office-furniture warehouse but still with its dress circle, the large projection box, and some thirties theatre decoration intact) once the films finish. They raced to High Street then Arthur Head which had everything a kid

Princess Chambers and Theatre, c1974.
[Michal Lewi]

Previous page: A grand new station for Fremantle, with glittering marble-tiled toilets, 1907.
[Fremantle City Library: Local History Collection]

needs to re-enact the just-seen film: cliffs with jagged rocks below, then the ocean; a castle or prison, lighthouse, caves, jetty, boats, everything.

Then the greatest excitement of all: Larry and his friends are swimming off Arthur Head in January 1945 and watch as the port goes up in black smoke. A welder on a Panamanian-registered rust-bucket, the *Panamanian,* throws a burning hessian bag into the water to extinguish it. Instead the oily water catches fire. Next, the water beneath North Wharf is ablaze, then the *Panamanian* itself. Next door is the British submarine tender *Maidstone* with its lethal cargo of torpedoes, warheads and oil. The port could be blown up — along with much of Fremantle. The *Panamanian* breaks free and drifts among the submarines but is pushed back against the wharf by tugs with brave crews. Those subs that can be moved head for the open sea, past Larry and his friends who are still in the water. The triggering explosion doesn't happen and Fremantle survives but it takes a week for the fire to be totally extinguished. My father who is officer-in-charge of the Department of Information releases the story for local papers. There has been a fire 'in an Australian port'. It wasn't hard to guess where that may have been from the oily black soot falling in Perth and Fremantle back yards.

On quieter days the war-time kids play cricket at the

Fremantle on the edge:
the Panamanian *on fire, 1945.*
[Fremantly History Collection: Local History Collection]

western end of High Street, with the tram crews from the terminus often joining in. One conductor never plays. He is George who drops off each trip, north, east or south, for a beer at the National and is picked up on the return trip. The trams are Fremantle's rumour mills, particularly during a war. One rumour is that George's beer money comes from collecting issued tickets from the tram floor, ironing them smooth overnight then re-selling them. Big boys sometimes watch the war — or at least the warriors — pass by while they stand in a queue stretching towards The Palms, the Bannister Street brothel. When they get close to the action there will always be an impatient American willing to swap a place in the queue for US dollars. The lads earn their money: when there's a troop convoy the queue can stretch up the full length of Bannister Street, along Market Street, and part of the way down Collie Street. Ron Warren is a teenager who is managing the family menswear business after his father goes to the war. The story around town is that he earns his pocket money standing in the Bannister Street queue. In 1977 he is Fremantle's deputy mayor.

We are back at the Fremantle Hotel, where High and Cliff Streets intersect, when I mention that my father and my father's friend, Jimmy James, Civilian Director Naval Intelligence Fremantle, used to gather information in the pub's saloon bar. This is where shipping company managers and, more importantly, skippers drink. The Royal Australian Navy, based in the Elder building, is not keen to pass intelligence across to their civilian employees so our dynamic duo quiz the attractive barmaid who provides a comforting ear to lonely skippers from neutral countries. 'That'd be the Duchess. Ships often left late because of her,' says Alec. Grace Connolly was the Dutchess; she had a stylish and very proper manner. I can tell Alec the saloon bar information was valued in high places. After my father died in 1996, I found among his papers a letter on official stationery from the Admiralty, Whitehall, London, dated September 1945. The Admiralty thank the Fremantle operatives for the 'quality of their intelligence, the sort which wins wars'.

Pubs like the Fremantle prosper after the Second World War. There is no shortage of pubs but there are plenty of drinkers to go around. Different maritime unions have different hotels where they 'get full' in the public bars each Friday. That does not, however, stop Alec's father George Smith standing outside his establishment to see that his drinkers are not sneaking across to the Orient. Clem Bahen from the Orient reciprocates. These are not sophisticated establishments in the 1950s but fifty years earlier many were. The closest you'll get in the fifties and sixties to a bottle of table red may be sweet sherry from the fridge. When the pubs shut at nine there's always a licensed club where you can drink till

Hotel Fremantle in the 1970s:
'naval intelligence centre', 1943.
[Brian Richards]

Wyola Club, 2006.
[Aaron Photographics]

eleven. The clubs are the real winners of the licensing system: the Wyola Club each week spikes more than fifty 18-gallon kegs. That's a lot of beer! Meanwhile, the less fortunate drink at the nearby Melbourne Wine Saloon in High Street. Some start at ten in the morning with a round of sweet sherry to secure some glasses then move on to serious drinking — metho and orange juice from bottles in brown paper bags hidden under the table. I know this because the wonderful storyteller Connie Herbert worked there and she recalls details of her customers with affection.

We cross High Street to the 1950s decor of the Roma restaurant to eat fried squid for lunch. I ask Nella Abrugiato whether the menu has changed much since she and husband Frank opened the Roma in 1954, when roast chicken and spaghetti is their signature dish and the chickens arrive live in cages. 'Well not really. Whenever we take a dish off the menu diners complain. It is their favourite: they've been having it most weeks for thirty years. So we don't change much.'

There's a small sign on the wall above the cash register announcing that roast chickens can be taken away for one pound. It is painted by NU SIGNS, the small business of a sign-writer with big ideas, Alan Bond, in the lane behind the restaurant. It's the company's first sign but the bouncy young sign-writer wants a prohibitive five pounds for it. Frank thinks:

'That's a lot of money for a very little sign. He's robbing me but what the heck. I need a sign.' Frank pays up. Later a famous Alan Bond signs the sign — for free. The building which housed NU SIGNS becomes the headquarters of the Waterside Workers Federation then the University of Notre Dame's College of Business. Irony piles upon irony.

We head east through the varied history of High Street. The street goes into physical decline in the mid-fifties when a delivery truck knocks over a support pole and an elaborate two-storey verandah crashes to the footpath. Other verandahs hit the deck and the Fremantle City Council decides they are a hazard to the busy crowds below. Large trucks deliver wool and other bulky goods through streets and into warehouses designed for horse-drawn drays. My immediate destination is the National Hotel, until recently one of the few workers' pubs left in Fremantle. Later it becomes the Nash and is painted a tacky blue and has a proprietor who throws out many of the old drinkers. Then a new owner removes the blue paint and starts to restore the verandahs, but will the drinkers return? The story of the National is one of Fremantle's strangest. It started in the 1880s with young William Conroy, a member of an Irish hotel family, converting a branch office of the National Bank into a hotel. When the Town Hall, which towers over all the surrounding buildings, opens on 22 June 1887, Conroy wants to join in the

High Street looking west, 1905:
the eight hour day celebrations.
[Fremantle City Library: Local History Collection]

Foundation Day lunch,
Fremantle Town Hall, 1929.
The invitation asked that gentlemen refrain from smoking because of the number of ladies attending.
[Fremantle City Library: Local History Collection]

evening's celebration — a fancy dress ball for children. But he hasn't a ticket and is drunk, or may be just a little crazy. The doorman, Councillor John Snook, turns him away.

Conroy goes back to the National and collects a small revolver. He returns, argues with Cr Snook, then shoots him in the mouth. The councillor is sixty-nine and he dies three months later. Did he actually die of old age? Is this murder? The jury says no to the first question and yes to the second and adds a strong recommendation for mercy. But the unpopular Governor Broome has just been burnt in effigy on High Street and is in no mood to do one of its residents a big favour by commuting the sentence to life imprisonment. Conroy's hanging is botched: he dies kicking. State executions are shifted from Perth to Fremantle as the Convict Establishment is transferred to state authorities. The sound of the gaol clock chiming eight on execution Monday mornings caused a shudder to run through many in the community for the next seventy-five years.

Like most of Fremantle, the National was rebuilt during the turn-of-the-century building spree, with a corner tower and brilliantly coloured glass in windows around the bar area. This is how it still looks when it provides the catalyst for the Battle of High Street. It is 1943 and the riotous New Zealand troops are passing through Fremantle. They rush out of the pub to jeer at a group of Americans who are in full kit and on a route march. This means they carry knives which normally are banned from Fremantle by service authorities. The aggravation gathers momentum inside the hotel. Two New Zealanders are fatally stabbed by Americans who have dropped off the march without permission. Soon six hundred New Zealanders, Americans and some British naval ratings are fighting up and down High Street. 'We asked for it and we got what we asked for,' says a wounded New Zealander as the two dead and several injured are taken away in a service truck. Next morning the *West Australian* reports the 'incident' in a single sentence. It happened 'somewhere in Australia'.

Opposite the National, one of Fremantle's major commercial enterprises begins. A would-be merchant arrives in 1853 with partner and two sons to open a bakery and cake shop. When the spouse dies in 1858 more income is needed to support a family which now comprises five children. An emporium is added, M Higham and Son, at the corner of High and Market Streets. The company diversifies from merchandise to the pastoral industry, then to pearling which can be a good earner. This is the typical upward path for a Fremantle Merchant Prince to follow. Only this prince is a princess — Mary Higham. The *West Australian* praises Mary on her retirement in 1880: 'It is seldom that we find an

The National Hotel, Market Street: waiting for the street war, c1940.
[Saxon Fogarty]

instance of a woman devoting herself to business in the energetic manner that Mrs Higham did.' The men admire her but there are commercial and political groups she can't join. Her son Edward, who leaves school at twelve to help his mother, deputises.

Mary Higham dies in 1883 but the enterprises continue to prosper as the population of Fremantle trebles in the years between the Yilgarn gold strikes and Federation, 1887–1901, and there is a great demand for clothing, furniture and tents. Then a slump follows from 1905 when the WA Government Railway Workshops are shifted from behind the present Fremantle Station to Midland — along with three hundred families. Some workers travel there each day on 'the rattler' which leaves at 6.00am. There are strict but unwritten rules about who sits in which seat on the trip to Midland. The government decision to move the workshops has other social ramifications. A cluster of five houses, strategically sited on the path from the port along Market and Phillimore Streets is demolished. Five brothel keepers and their staff are sad and look for sites in Perth and Kalgoorlie.

You may wonder how it is that the opulent buildings of Fremantle's West End survive while an attractive continental boulevard like St Georges Terrace in Perth becomes a glass, concrete and steel wind-tunnel. The mineral boom entrepre-

Storms took heavy toll on Fremantle's tired 1860s cottages, 1923.
[A Orloff]

Previous page: Fremantle's first railway station, at the river end of Mouat Street — but it wrecked the Fremantle Green.
[The Battye Library — 10008P]

Sustenance workers outside Stammers store in East Fremantle during the Depression.
[Fremantle Society Collection]

neurs and property developers don't see a big killing to be made in Fremantle and mostly stay away. However, there is another threat the Fremantle City Council as developer. In the fifties and sixties 'Modernism' is thought to be essential to the city's economic survival. Thousands of new blue-collar workers are expected to arrive in Fremantle driving cars and trucks and requiring widened roads. The Fremantle City Council builds new offices in 1962 and then the Westgate development, which involves the destruction of attractive dwellings and small businesses. Council was enthusiastic and in 1972 the Myer/Woolworths project arrives. But there are more than economic reasons for this brutality. Old buildings remind many councillors of the Depression: of barefoot kids scrounging food on the wharf, hungry families, drunks in the gutter, tramps sleeping around the waterfront, and lots of grime and peeling paint. They say Fremantle must modernise or become an industrial slum. In the 1960s Mayor 'Mr Fremantle' Fred Samson sees Fremantle becoming not a slum but a well-planned industrial area. Inner city terraces are not favoured. 'People bring the rats,' the mayor tells me.

The city loses its grand entrance of two-storey mansions which had lined Queen Victoria Street, with their stunning interior jarrah panelling, fine stonework and gardens backing down to the river. They become car yards. The press calls the modernisers ‘the progressives’, which riles their opponents. The opposing viewpoint comes strongly from a wide range of establishment and union figures, but mainly from members of the resident action group, the Fremantle Society, which begins in 1972.

The first bout between the modernisers and their opponents begins in 1973 with a proposal to build a sixteen-storey ‘glass gothic tower’ at the north-eastern corner of Queen and Adelaide Streets, near the Town Hall. The protagonists claim the tower will become the ‘tourist attraction of the southern hemisphere.’ The Fremantle Society sees the port city becoming sterile, like Perth. The conflict becomes intense and personal. A strangled rooster is left on the Ellen Street doorstep of the feisty founder of the Fremantle Society, Les Lauder. Death threats are made against him and the police are called in. The sixteen storeys drop to eight, and then to four, under the rising public disapproval of the developer’s tactics.

Round two takes place in 1974 at a Fremantle City Council meeting. The ‘progressives’ want to pull down the Evan Davies Library building, home of the state’s first free municipal library, which occupies a triangle of land between South Terrace and Market Street. It is still the Fremantle Literary Institute in the late 1920s when a barefoot twelve-year-old, Kim Beazley Senior, later to become Federal Minister for

Les Lauder, left, takes Commonwealth Environment Minister, Moss Cass, to inspect the threatened 1880s Court House on Marine Terrace, 1974.

[Les Lauder]

Education, walks from his home in King William Street, South Fremantle. He ascends the jarrah staircase, passes the amber stair-window, and enters the hushed, very formal library area where he borrows English literary periodicals for his father Alf, who works on the wharf. Kim reads them all the way back to his home — as you'd expect.

The old library will become a feature of the cappuccino strip, housing the Dome. Gino's is Gino's Suit Hire. In 1974, however, both are destined to become a car park. 'Fire a shotgun down South Terrace and you wouldn't hit anyone,' says Sadie Stone, a no-nonsense pro-demolition councillor. She is probably right. The conservationist councillors don't think they have the numbers to stop it when Fremantle's mayor, Bill McKenzie — a Labor Party insider known for political savvy — puts a complex motion crafted the night before by himself and the city manager Stan Parks. He counts the raised hands. Motion carried. He quickly turns to the next agenda item. The audience looks glum. Fremantle as they know it and like it seems finished. What some don't realise is that a yes vote stops the building being demolished. It is possible that some of the 'progressives' also didn't realise that when they raised their hands. Someone mutters: 'The one-arm bandit strikes again.' McKenzie carries his left arm in a black silk sling following childhood polio. Every council vote on demolition or

Fremantle Literary Institute, 1908:
threatened by the wreckers in 1974.
Now the Dome Cafe, with Kulcha,
a multicultural arts venue,
on the first floor.
[Fremantle City Library: Local History Collection]

The classical survivor:
Victoria Hall, 2003.
[Michal Lewi]

development proposals — frequently for car parks — becomes a close and bitter battle as the number of 'new' councillors increases.

The knockout — or what seemed like the knockout at the time — happens in round three, outside Victoria Hall, an Anglican hall and later one of Fremantle's many dance venues. Only two years earlier its neighbour, the art deco cinema Oriana, has been demolished without protest except from a few academics who claim that to watch an Elvis Presley film from the theatre's front row on a Saturday afternoon is one of life's joys. The Oriana is replaced by shops.

Victoria Hall has a wonderfully detailed facade and a timber-vaulted ceiling which, if you direct your voice at the appropriate point, responds like a musical instrument. It is owned by band leader and barber, Norm Wrightson ('Six chairs, no waiting'), and his brother, Robert, the world ballroom dancing champion. They wanted to see it demolished — as people did in 1974. Bob Olsen is an organiser with the Builders Labourers. He is no favourite with building contractors who seem to like to punch his face — which is both tough and urbane — or to hit it with a shovel. Bob wants to save Victoria Hall by having a Green Ban placed on it, which would prevent any re-development on the site. But he'd like to see strong community support before the union stepped in. It is 10.00pm when he sets about massaging that support. He plasters his blond hair with soot and darkens his face, which is often dusty anyhow; he puts on safety boots and glasses and a hard hat. The number plates of his Simca and trailer are obscured with flour dough. He then throws some picks and shovels on to the trailer and heads for the hall. Once there he leans the tools against the front door and flashes his torch. 'Get that flooring up. The truck will be here soon', he shouts into the empty hall. A woman passerby hears that and screams, 'Get Les (Lauder).' There's panic on the footpath. The mystery demolisher decides to, as he puts it, POQ. Next morning, at a Builders Labourers stop work meeting, Bob successfully moves for a green ban to be slapped on the hall. He mentions community support.

Later in the day Bob is sitting in one of Norm's six chairs. Norm is trimming the back of his neck with a cut-throat razor. As he trims, Norm also talks with a customer in the next chair. He says what he'd do if he could get his hands on those unionists. Bob starts to sweat as the glistening razor runs over his neck.

A big crowd gathers outside Victoria Hall for the auction. This is an important sale because any new building will be set back as part of the scheme to widen High Street, as was done

Norm (Six chairs, no waiting)
Wrightson, c1983.
[Daniel Bruyn]

with shops on the Oriana site. The sale seems to have been made and the hammer about to drop when Tony Henry, another organiser from the Builders Labourers Federation shuffles from the crowd. There is a green ban on Victoria Hall, he announces. The unspoken message is that it will be difficult to erect a replacement building on that site. The crowd of conservation supporters claps then breaks up. Some are overjoyed: others from the more respectable suburbs are perturbed by the use of union muscle, or rather the promise *not* to use their muscles.

Two seminal events along South Terrace help promote the Cappuccino Strip's development in the seventies. In 1977 Nunzio Gumina buys Papa Luigi's Coffee and Pizza Lounge at the corner of Collie Street, complete with its pinball machines. It's a place where, by day, old men sit over strong black coffees and talk of Sicily and fishing. At night the hoons move in. If you fired Sadie's shotgun down South Terrace you'd probably hit a rumbling Holden Monaro or Chrysler Charger. Sometimes their drivers will stop with their radios thumping, roll their sleeves even more tightly into their armpits and joust with the jeering pinball players.

Nunzio understands hoons: he has done 'bog laps' of Fremantle Town Hall in an FJ Holden crammed with half a dozen of his friends, in the days before the High Street mall.

Corner of Collie and South Terrace:
Clegg's furniture store, 1905,
becomes Papa Luigi's, 1978.
[Fremantle City Library: Local History Collection / Michal Lewi]

The town centre, 1975. High Street leading up to Kings Square and the Town Hall at top, and Market Street running into South Terrace across the bottom.
[Fremantle City Library: Local History Collection]

He puts tables out onto the footpath and makes the hoons sit on chairs: they want to hunker on the windowsill. He serves them black coffee: they want cappuccino. The persistent late-night encounters between Fremantle and out-of-town hoons is solved in a number of ritualistic jousts which Nunzio referees, in an empty cellar under the cafe. He has heard the boys from Coolbellup are coming to beat up the locals that evening. Nunzio prepares with borrowed boxing equipment. The ring is slung between four of the massive twenty-five centimetre jarrah struts which support the cellar roof. When they arrive the combatants are led downstairs. Nine bouts are fought between representatives of the two groups: the Marquess of Queensberry comes to Fremantle. Problem solved, Nunzio is now ready to concentrate on his dream — al fresco dining.

Perth critics say eating outside will draw the flies. It certainly draws the people: the Orange People, followers of Bhagwan Shree Rajneesh who seem about to take over the city; smart local people; the international smart people here for the America's Cup; a murderer or two and endless mad philosophers. The current licensing laws are a problem for Nunzio, but only briefly. He introduces Three Beans to the strip. All you have to do is say 'three beans' and a small white cup appears, containing deadly Sambucca with three coffee beans floating in the clear viscous fluid. The police do nothing. They

Nunzio Gumina, one of the best known faces in Fremantle, looking slightly saturnine.
[Daniel Bruyn]

are not being bribed. It is only when other restaurants obtain licences to allow alcohol to be served on the footpath that three beans disappears from South Terrace. The pinball players are replaced by artists like Sam Abercrombie and Ben Joel who paint murals featuring staff on a curling wave of cappuccino. Sam and others are also painting the mural above the proscenium arch of His Majesty's Theatre in Perth. They take turns at acting as models: Fremantle identity Aurora Morelli, Sam's girlfriend at the time, is Morning. Things must have changed since Fremantle boys threw stones at her but it isn't clear whether it was because she was a girl or an Italian.

Across at 50 Market Street another event in Fremantle's shift from industrial centre to a place of entertainment occurs in 1979. The Market Street Book Arcade arrives, with the help, it is said, of some funding from John Troy. It is run by the Socialist Labour League (SLL) and advertises that it is 'the Australian publisher of Trotsky'. There can't have been much competition from bookshops wanting to make such a claim. The shop sells Russian science books, relationship books, political books and, perhaps rashly, world bestsellers. It is open from 8.30am to 11.30pm which gives residents and visitors something to do after the usual 5.30 closing time. Late at night they may find there a goddess of the Left, Vanessa Redgrave perhaps. Captivated men wearing black caps and conspiratorial

South Terrace, 1905, with the opera house balcony in the right foreground.
[Jamelia Gubgub]

looks provide a backdrop. Market Street Books leaves its mark on Fremantle trading habits before ideological purging — probably over the sale of bestsellers — and the departure of SLL principal Bill Dellar, cause its downfall. 'This is a red raggers' town,' says Alan Bond. It is less so after Market Street Books leave. Bob's Shoe Shop takes over the site.

Further south, beside the Freemasons Hotel (now the Sail and Anchor), Fremantle has its own opera house. The Dalkeith Opera House is built in 1904 for James Gallop and features Renaissance architecture, a richly decorated auditorium seating 1200, with another 300 in the gallery. When the densely ornamented ventilators can't handle the summer temperature the roof is rolled back to reveal the stars. Opera patrons parade on the balcony over South Terrace in their late-Victorian gear, the women wearing silks and satins in rich colours. Silent movies will make things difficult for live theatre and it soon becomes the King's Theatre. In fact, it may have opened as the King's Theatre, however, the Gallop family always called it the Dalkeith Opera House. By 1905, on the King's Theatre balcony there's an event to aid Fremantle Hospital with Fisher Beard and Company showing 'wonderful designs in trimmed millinery'. Another balcony showing the same year is a fundraiser for injured South Fremantle footballers.

Victor Gubgub remembers seeing Nellie Melba at the

Fashion on High Street. John and Sheree Dornan, Love in Tokyo, 2006
[Aaron Photographics]

Ford's the fashion on South Terrace, Victor Motors, c1955.
[Jamelia Gubgub]

theatre in 1914 when he was seven. He became a pioneer advocate for physical fitness and taught boxing in the cavernous building during the war. In 1946 he purchases it and opens a Ford dealership, Victor Motors. The windows sparkle with new cars inside as Fords grow teeth. Howard Porter Motors is then just up the road and the two showrooms have a saw doctor and Jack 'Tinny' Thomas's ginger-beer stall between them. Across the road is a noisy woodyard. Each Christmas Victor hosts a special lunch for his hundred and thirty employees at the Freemasons'. It's a slap-up affair but to be admitted the workers must do a fitness run via the Town Hall to get there. Furtive figures in overalls creep across the lane between the two buildings.

The Opera House which maybe never was, is now the Metropolis Night Club and is divided into five chambers apparently following Chinese philosophy: fire, metal, earth, water and air. The balcony, which was restored in 2002 on the basis of fragments of old photos and Victor's long-term memory, hangs over busy South Terrace: it is part of Chamber 5, air. There was some doubt whether the balustrade columns were turned wood or cast iron. Working drawings are taken to Victor, then ninety-five, who rules in favour of cast iron. Joe Madaffari, one of three Calabrian brothers who manage Metropolis, tells me the patrons sitting on the balcony are

Gino's
Trattoria
Coca-Cola
BENNY'S GELATI
THE BEST of them all!
Heineken

older and quieter than those clubbing inside: 'They're about twenty-three.' The women wear low-rise jeans, bare midriffs, almost transparent petticoat tops, bejewelled navels, and kitten heels: the men can't wear aggressive boots. Other young people are in the streets or selling things from doorways as the clubbers pass. A wide-eyed young woman sitting on the footpath selling 'hemp jewellery' nods towards the clubbers and tells me that they must have a job. She adds that Fremantle is not a bad place to be young and poor. Nearby, Nigel wears a black beanie and a very sad look. He sits cross-legged in a doorway with a sign: NO MONEY NO FOOD NO HOME NO HOPE. He is approached by two of the largest police I've seen. They talk with him: he disappears.

Joe Madaffari says alternative rocker John Butler was busking outside Metropolis in 2000. He builds up a crowd which starts to block the club's entrance. The managing director, Mario Madaffari, asks him — nicely — to go and perform somewhere else. This he does. Twelve months later he is a big star with a number one hit and appears inside Metropolis to a sell-out crowd.

It is difficult to imagine that a hundred years ago this stretch of South Terrace houses wall-to-wall Chinese greengrocers and grocers who provide for a multicultural and migrant community. They sell four-gallon tins of kerosene to those

View from the Metropolis verandah, 2005.
[Joe Madaffari]

Previous page: Gino's, South Terrace, waiting for the America's Cup, 1984.
[Aaron Photographics]

John Butler at the Fremantle Markets.
[John Butler]

needing heat and light. These tins, beaten flat, provide walls for stables and back sheds, and reflectors for lamps on carts. Further south, in Suffolk Street and Bannister Street, more specialised traders are selling opium.

On the Henderson Street corner is a hotel whose provenance includes familiar names — Australia, Freemasons', Sail and Anchor. During the Second World War it was Freemasons'. The lessee Fred Day dies in 1942. Fights between US and Australian servicemen who might also be Australian husbands, visits by American shore patrols with black batons the length of a baseball bat, and shortages of bar staff make running a war-time hotel potentially lethal. The new manager, Merton Day, Fred's son, arrives with his wife Emelda from their home in Dalkeith. Merton has grown up in a hotel family although he manages a Perth shoe shop. He is happy enough with the switch; for Emelda it's a bit of a shock. Both will be on any list of Fremantle's legendary pub-keepers before they leave the hotel. Merton is a sweetie. He reaches for his wallet once he hears a hard-luck story starting. He hears plenty. These handouts take place in the front bar where the walls are covered with team photos of the great South Fremantle sides. The faces he sees on the walls will line the bar most evenings. South has no licensed club until 1957. South supporters race from Fremantle Oval at half-time to down three or four quick

Freemasons' Hotel, where The Book *was burned, 1949.*
[E Lewis; Fremantle City Library: Local History Collection]

Following page: Organ loft at St Patrick's.
[Daniel Bruyn]

middies; most hurry back to catch the third quarter, refreshed.

Merton dies of cancer in 1959. Emelda Day takes over the lease and with it the problem of *The Book.* It is a delicate problem. *The Book* is a nondescript, black-covered volume with indented letters down the side. It records years of debts chalked up by hotel patrons. The maritime unions can be sensitive about their members being hounded for payment — and they provide a lot of business. One evening Emelda Day walks into the front bar carrying *The Book.* Holding it above her head she announces: 'I know it's not Christmas but I'm giving you all a present.' *The Book* goes into the fire. Emelda Day soon discovers the maritime unions can also support her. A seaman arrives in the front bar. He tells her Merton died while he was at sea, and owes him £200 over a shared bet on a horse. That's a big bet in 1960. Mrs Day consults a seaman friend who questions the claimant then rules the alleged bet is decidedly dodgy. The seaman approaches the optimistic punter: 'Don't ever work on a ship sailing out of Fremantle. We'll have to throw you overboard.'

Mrs Day gradually takes control of her hotel and her male patrons, although she can never bring herself to travel with the male darts team for their away matches at other pubs. But she does send money to buy drinks all round.

Some things about her pub Mrs Day can never understand,

like why local detectives turn up on Fridays to collect a box of crays each from fishermen. For what could this be a pay-off? It's difficult to imagine. It remains a mystery. In the sixties, the Swan Brewery which owns the hotel decides to tidy up. Out come the attractive pressed tin walls and ceilings; the delicately curving section of the front bar, where the Victor Motors salesmen seal deals on Fords, is brutally straightened. Mrs Day leaves and says she will never return to see the damage. I meet her in 1993. She has come to Fremantle from her home in Bicton for Monday Mass at Saint Patrick's: she objects to having to go to Mass on Sundays. Has she been to see her hotel, now called the Sail and Anchor? I tell her the pressed tin is reinstated, and the rich colours; the bars are polished rather than painted and a small brewery is producing boutique beers. I say I think she'd like it. I don't think she ever returned.

Walk around the Sail and Anchor corner and there is Ma Xinhua, 'the Chinese professional artist'. Ma has been drawing there for the last dozen years. He uses charcoal and attracts custom from mothers with infants. The infant is screaming yet Ma Xinhua's sketch has her absolutely serene; likewise the fraught mother. The artist's repertoire of famous faces has been increasing along the pub wall: Madonna, Elvis, John Wayne, Bruce Lee, Shane Warne, Ned Kelly, Don Bradman … Have the Don's eyes taken on just a touch of the Asian or am I

Warders' Cottages, c1974.
[Michal Lewi]

imagining it? In the square between the hundred-year-old markets and the hotel you can buy a bird whistle for a dollar or watch international buskers before they fly off for the European summer. Buskers talk about the space as 'the best pitch in the world' in the way fast bowlers once refered to the WACA. On Sunday mornings a dozen or so of the top performers draw from a hat for one-hour time-slots on the Markets pitch where the record 'hat' is $1000. This is obviously someone with a good 'crowd draw' and good 'hat lines'. All of this happens against the austere backdrop of the Prison Warders' Cottages (now public housing) built in the early 1850s. The Comptroller of Convicts, Colonel E Y B Henderson, rents a house when he arrives in 1850 and is shocked at the cost. So he makes accommodation for his staff a priority and also built The Knowle for himself and his young wife Mary in 1856. She dies soon after.

Press on to Fremantle Oval, the home of South Fremantle Football Club and for half a century East Fremantle. The rivalry between the two clubs is still fierce and makes it difficult to create the Dockers as a team in the national competition with an intense local following. But a passionate dislike of the Eagles — the Perth team — becomes another force: 'If the Eagles were playing in my back yard I'd draw the curtains,' a Dockers' supporter tells me. 'I'd lower the clothes' hoist a few inches

If it happened in Fremantle, it probably happened at Fremantle Oval. A carnival in 1905.
[Fremantle City Library: Local History Collection]

first,' another one says. The oval started as a parade ground for the pensioner guards and was known as the Barracks Green Field. The original Fremantle Football Club moves in during 1895. It was thought, wrongly, that an oval with an internal fence would constrain violence between players and onlookers. 1895 was a violent year and Fremantle loses the financial support needed to pay its star players from Victoria and South Australia. In 1900 South Fremantle takes over.

The asymmetrical green space that was Fremantle Oval was defined by a bumpy cycle track which is dangerous for footballers and cycle racers who include a small number of women. Horace 'Horry' Marshall, champion of that track and the road, becomes as famous as any Fremantle footballer after he beats Hubert Opperman in the 1926 Warrnambool to Melbourne cycle race. He's accustomed to rough rides. Like many of the footballers he drives a truck on the wharf. These are not recent vehicles but salvage from the First World War — they have solid rubber tyres.

The playing surface at Fremantle Oval breathes symbiotically with the port (as do many aspects of Fremantle life). The big union meetings are held there. In the thirties, forties and fifties, most Fremantle footballers work on the wharf. Lumping heavy cargoes leaves them physically strong; their union affiliation leaves them suitably truculent. When they are on strike most arrive early on their bikes (usually a Swansea) for training, although some may be lost while passing a waterside hotel. If there's a late shift players may not train at all, or will train in the dark.

South start their time at the top in 1947, taking over from East Fremantle with whom they have a love/hate relationship; they share opposite ends of Fremantle Oval. South's new coach, Ross Hutchinson, has no coaching staff: he is coach of everything plus an amateur sports psychologist. His major helper, Frank Harrison, secretary and recruiting officer, stands at the rear of the Fremantle press box with his back to the game listening to his portable radio. He's almost blind and can't see the play. The coach is a distinguished sort of chap, having acquired considerable gloss since he came up from the tiny timber town of Dean Mill to go to an expensive private boarding school. He has won a Distinguished Flying Cross for coaxing the tattered remnants of a Lancaster bomber across occupied Europe before landing safely in Britain — to the cheers of his crew. At the oval his language remains heroic. In his address to his players gathered in the gloom and tobacco smoke and heavy smells of massage oil beneath the old Victoria Pavilion, the coach may quote from Kipling's tales of the Raj: when a comeback is needed he calls on Herodotus and paraphrases his account of the battle between the Greeks and the Persians five centuries before

Expensive Victorian import, Tom O'Dea, kicks his first goal for Fremantle, 1896. This photograph of Fremantle Oval may be the oldest surviving action image of Western Australian football.

[Beatel and Williams]

Christ. Lumpers and truck drivers in the team may wonder about this well-spoken, charming man, the more so when he stands as a Liberal Party candidate in 1948 for a Legislative Council seat based on Fremantle. But there's never a smirk. These men may dislike the bosses but they will never question their coach, even if he is destined to become a Liberal Party minister and Speaker in State Parliament — and Sir Ross.

The Fremantle tribal culture was complex and male and unreasonable. Pearl Smith, in *A Small Fish,* provides a series of sad glimpses of life on the edge of this culture. She marries Jock Smith, working-class hero and eventually national president of the Waterside Workers Federation. Pearl calls her husband Jack, never Jock. She thought Jock was a pretentious name which smacked of British trade unionism. She speaks without rancour: 'Jack married the wrong girl and I certainly married the wrong bloke. I loved music and dancing. He loved pubs and mates. All we had in common was growing up in homes without love.'

South is arguably the champion of Australia in the early 1950s with a truck driver from South Fremantle taking over as coach. They thrash the top Victoria sides both at home and away. But this day South, at home, lose by a few points which directs the crowd's attention to the umpire. Today it's the infuriatingly immaculate Ray Montgomery who has to walk

'My football career was like Joseph's coat', Ross Hutchinson — premiership coach of East Fremantle, West Perth and South Fremantle — liked to say.

[A Orloff]

Ray Montgomery.
[Alan East]

through a hostile crowd without any protection apart from two young police officers. Monty is a Midland Railway Workshops coach builder who has become an art teacher. That's enough to make him suspect in working-class Fremantle.

Squelch!

An orange hits Monty in the chest from close range. A ripe stain spreads across his whiter-than-white shirt. The two young police officers turn to chase the offender. They seem to have him trapped against the rusting perimeter fence. There is no escape. Then the crowd forms a protective circle. Deftly placed feet catch the police mid-stride while the offender is shouldered over the fence. One of the officers picks himself up, bleeding from lacerations to his face and arms following his tumble on the sharp stones embedded in the bitumen paving. 'I'm from Fremantle too,' he complains. Yes, but you're a copper.

With the arrival of machinery on the wharf and the drop in the number of players who work there, South's hard-man image fades. Their coach John Todd — the golden boy of the fifties whose genius was blighted by a knee injury in the days before joint reconstructions — laments the change. Standing in front of the Victoria Pavilion in the 1980s he says: 'We don't have any mongrel in us; that's our problem. East Fremantle have plenty of mongrel.'

How do the Dockers fit into this picture, composed as it is

of local heroes? They have made a pitch for a less exalted following than the affluent Eagles, and Fremantle stars of the fifties come to demonstrate the beautiful but lost art of the dropkick. But their supporters come from everywhere, as do their players who wear thousand dollar designer suits rather than the blue cardigans of old and drive expensive cars to the game rather than take the team bus. The Dockers are a corporation, just as all AFL teams are. But with a difference. A brothel keeper is a corporate sponsor and the team's well-equipped massage room is named after her: The Mary-Anne Kenworthy room. I am travelling by train to a Dockers game at Subiaco. A passenger says, 'I bet more Dockers' barrackers get on at Cottesloe and Claremont than at Fremantle'. He's probably right. And just to display his Fremantle bona fides he tells me how in the thirties he used to stand on the pedestrian bridge, now gone, behind Fremantle Station, with his legs apart, and let the engine blow steam up his shorts.

Leave Fremantle Oval and walk up the Ramp which leads to the prison. The Ramp is composed of limestone spoil, the result of quarrying and the construction of the main cell block of the Convict Establishment between 1851 and 1859. In 1868 the Irish Fenian prisoner John Boyle O'Reilly moves up the Ramp and so do nearly ten thousand other male convicts who arrive in Fremantle between 1850 and 1868. The poet-revolutionary

John Gerovich's famous mark in 1956, now set in bronze by Robert Hitchcock. Fremantle Oval's 1890s Victoria Pavilion is in the background.

[Aaron Photographics]

blinks at the dusty whiteness of the roadway and of the main cell block and wonders how quickly he can get away. He does escape and is subsequently involved in a plan to free six of the remaining Fenian prisoners who were transported for their part in the unsuccessful uprising in 1867. In 1876 a conspirator with the *Catalpa*, an American whaler sent to carry out the rescue, takes time off from carousing with the chambermaid at Patrick Moloney's Emerald Isle Hotel (now the Orient) and comes up the Ramp to inspect the prison on the invitation of William Robert Fauntleroy, the acting Comptroller General of the Convict Establishment. The plan to get the six Fenian prisoners away is then fine-tuned. The escape is successful, after a celebrated sea chase. The *Fremantle Herald* of 22 April reported:

> … *pensioners* [pensioner guards] *and the police felt they had been taking part in a very silly farce, and had been laughed at by the Yankees at sea and the public onshore.*

Former Australian Prime Minister Gough Whitlam is visiting the main cell block as patron of the Fremantle Society in 1994, in recognition of the part played by his government in the preservation of key elements of the port city's heritage twenty years earlier. He looks at the gallows, then turns away: 'This is a black place but we need such places.' More than

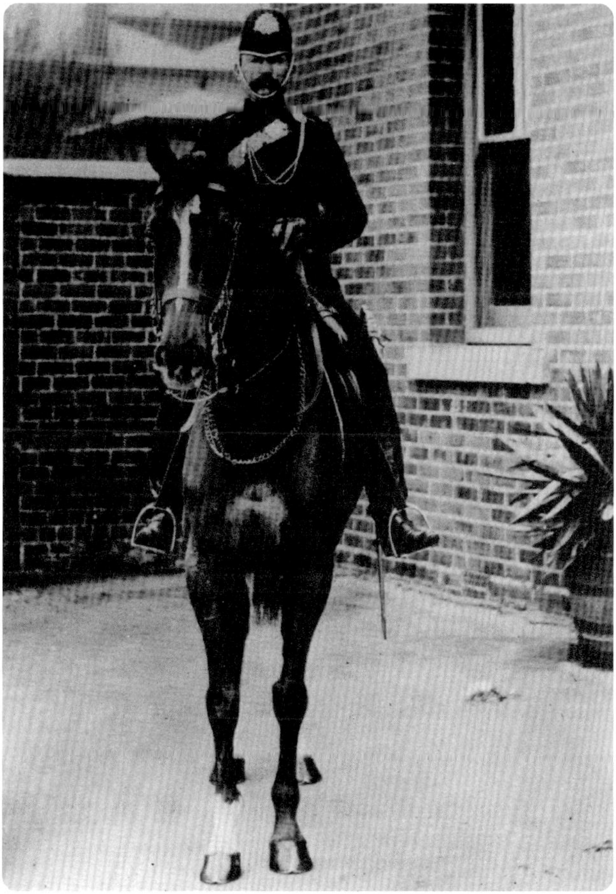

Thomas Rowe, a detective sergeant from Scotland Yard, accompanied the Fenian prisoners to Fremantle in 1868. He settled in the colony, becoming head of the Detective Branch of the local police force.

[John Rowe; Fremantle Prison Museum]

Former Prime Minister Gough Whitlam, as Patron of the Fremantle Society, visiting Fremantle Prison with Fremantle Mayor Jenny Archibald and, at right, Society President Ralph Hoare and member Ron Davidson, 1994.
[Michael Wearne]

Previous page: Prisoners on parade, Fremantle Prison, 1976.
[Michal Lewi]

12,800 lashes were administered during the years of convictism here after the benign reign of Colonel Henderson. Fenian prisoner Thomas McCarthy Fennell records what a flogging is like: 'With each lash the laceration seems to change from blue to intense black, the flesh tears apart, 'tis now red, and ghastly flow the purple fluids from the mangled pulp.' The myth persists that this was a happy time. Gough makes his farewells. He moves across to where a security man stands stiffly. He shakes hands very formally. 'I hope they let you out soon.'

There is humour about the place; grim humour. 'Go on, make my day,' a bored guard writes on a gun-tower wall. In the thirties, Ernest 'Shiner' Ryan, Australia's first armed robber to use a car for a hold-up in 1914, produces counterfeit coins from the prison workshops which the superintendent passes at the Freemasons' Hotel. Shiner also makes shimmering model sailing boats from surplus porridge and ground glass, and keeps the prison clock running on time. He goes straight, and becomes a Fremantle folk hero. His marriage at St John's to Kate Leigh, Sydney's Queen of the Underworld, is the social event of 1950. Shiner will not hear of anyone but Canon Edward Collick marrying them. He has been prison chaplain but is under suspension for sneaking out prisoners' letters without submitting them for inspection. At the same time an enterprising telephone technician, in prison for stealing copper

St John's and the Town Hall, c1940.
[Fremantle City Library: Local History Collection]

wire, somehow steals a phone and connects it to the official circuit. He rings the guard on the gun tower above him: 'Watch the southern wall. I think someone's trying to break out.' Then he clambers over the northern wall with a rope made from plaited sheets and a grappling iron crafted from the handle of a lavatory bucket.

A number of Fremantle Italians find themselves in Fremantle Prison after Italy sides with Germany in 1940. Both the grandfather and the father of Mayor Peter Tagliaferri do time there. Grandfather Pietro Tagliaferri is interned first. Peter's father Osvaldo (Aussie) answers the call and goes to join the Australian Army — but only if Pietro is released. The army doesn't agree and Aussie is gaoled for disobeying the order to enlist. The prison is closed in 1991 with physical conditions for prisoners having changed little over 135 years. It was this prison which caught the eye of Victorian novelist Anthony Trollope during a visit in 1872. He idolises the novelist William Makepeace Thackeray but discovers there are not too many Thackerays in Fremantle. He dismisses the town and its residents, in his travel journal *Australia*:

> *Fremantle has certainly no natural beauties to recommend it. It is a hot, white, ugly town, with a very large prison, a lunatic asylum, and a hospital for ancient and worn-out*

convicts ... At Fremantle there is hardly a man whom it can be worth the reader's while to have introduced to him.

Follow the path the Prison Surgeon used from his fine Georgian residence at No. 18 The Terrace, to the lunatic asylum. Follow the Prison wall up Fothergill Street then along Hampton Road. You are walking over an extensive system of drives and shafts cut by prisoners into a limestone aquifer twenty-five metres below to provide Fremantle with a safe water supply after a number of typhoid scares. Fremantle storytellers will tell you that one of the shafts runs up from Arthur Head. Convicts disembark and are put in a rowing boat which takes them under the town and they reappear in the middle of the Convict Establishment. Others will tell you that a tunnel runs south under Hampton Road to the Beaconsfield Hotel. Neither story is true although a horse-drawn tramway did run from South Jetty and the Commissariat, around Marine Terrace, up Essex Street, Henderson Street and the Ramp to the prison, and it did carry convicts and their provisions.

You pass three handsome turn-of-the-century houses in Ord Street, Nos 24, 20–22 and 18. George Seddon, local resident and chronicler of the area, provides a detailed commentary of the verandah of No. 24:

Ord Street, 1902.
[Fremantle Society Collection]

Fremantle always attracted crowds to fires and accidents. Here a tram has run off the rails into a High Street residence, killing an occupant. The house of chief warder Henry Blinco is at the top of the hill, on the corner with Hampton Road.
[Fremantle City Library: Local History Collection]

The verandah is supported by very tall and slender cast iron posts with a 'barley sugar' fluting, a slightly swollen base like an unopened water lily (an Egyptian motif) and small floral capitals. They were made in Fremantle …

Lionel Holdsworth, the immaculate accountant who always wears spats, spreads himself among the houses overlooking the prison in Ord Street. He arrives in Fremantle in 1868 on the last convict ship, the *Hougoumont.* He's a white-collar criminal with a twenty-year sentence for insurance fraud after he scuttles one of his ships. By 1879 he's a ticket-of-leave man and is soon on his way, making money and developing investment properties. In the late 1880s he has built his home Braeside, a mansion with limestone walls almost half a metre thick and a much-photographed garden. The sole remnant of Braeside is the back wall of limestone standing at the south-west corner of the intersection of High Street and Hampton Road. Next come four investment properties, all still standing — Nos 12, 14, 16 and 18. When Holdsworth dies in 1901 the serious burghers on the Fremantle Council make an ironical statement about their values. They change Doonan Street — which honours Joseph Doonan, the Assistant Superintendent of Fremantle Prison — to Holdsworth Street, commemorating one of Doonan's wealthy guests. Doonan was so affected by the

Catalpa incident that he cut his throat with a bread knife, but not fatally.

The south-east corner where High Street meets Hampton Road is where Ivanhoe, a stunning single-storey mansion, was built for James Lilly in 1889. A solitary fence pillar four metres high provides a clue to the scale of the house and garden. The Merchant Princes are becoming very rich and moving from the inner city to large conspicuous houses on prominent blocks on the edge of town. Ivanhoe is typical. Until 2005 it was a nondescript block of sixties flats and a disused service station turned car wash. Because of their size and position the grand houses come down in the sixties and early seventies, leaving the occasional grand fence and marble steps at the front of a block of flats. (See 5 Knutsford Street for an example.)

Stagger up High Street to Monument Hill Park. It's called Obelisk Hill in the nineteenth century when sea captains steer by a large obelisk erected near where the monument now stands. Nyungars watch the beach from here whenever a whale is being butchered. They will come down to feed on the scraps, their own sources of food being increasingly diminished by the settlement and then farming. Later, in the 1890s, Obelisk Hill is the centre of a canvas town housing new arrivals en route to Kalgoorlie. They are a boisterous, untidy lot and nearby residents object in a petition to council that their locality is

Ivanhoe, home of shipping prince, James Lilly, and later Captain Biddles. On this day in November 1916, Biddles and his wife, Blanche, were hosts to fifty orphans from Perth Girls' Orphanage. Ivanhoe was demolished in 1966 to make way for a block of flats and a service station.
[Fremantle City Library: Local History Collection]

being 'converted into a species of Pandemonium. Minor details like cleanliness and ordinary morality are ignored.' There are other encampments of twenty or thirty tents in the big back yards scattered around the town.

Move on in time to November 1940. The RAN's glamour cruiser *Sydney* fails to return from what seemed a routine escort run. For Fremantle this is a very personal loss. The ship is based in the port and many of the 645 missing men have families and friends here. Each morning wives, lovers, and mothers and children gather at the monument and wait for signs of the ship returning. Sculptor Greg James' *Sydney* memorial, marking sixty years since its sinking, captures this scene in bronze. The 'church' opposite is Fremantle Grammar School, an example of Fremantle Gothic Revival built in 1885. Henry Briggs is battling up through the limestone dust to his school. He's a large and ponderous man who is headmaster from 1882 to 1895. He has what seem like strange ideas in his head: that the philosophy of British education needs to be modified to make it relevant for the colonies. Fremantle's elite come to believe that too and also that their sons do not have to be sent to Britain for an education. In 1896 he enters parliament as the member for Western Province: a quite different successor to Harry Marshall, the raucous baker, brewer and fighter at football games. Briggs moves to the top

Fremantle could be a dangerous place for ships. It became safer when captains could steer by the Obelisk, a navigational aid built in 1867 on what is now Monument Hill. It was demolished in 1924.
[Fremantle City Library: Local History Collection]

Fremantle from Monument Hill, 1896.
[The Battye Library — BA1116/17]

of an even steeper street, Fothergill Street; our street. I looked over his house, as Fremantle people do, seventy years later. Why were there piles of bones buried in his back yard? Could a later tenant have been stealing sheep from the Robb Jetty abattoirs and butchering them in the back yard? One certainly worked there. There was also the strange design with doors in the western wall going nowhere. Did Sir Henry expect to marry and was leaving room for expansion? We wondered.

West of Fremantle Grammar at No. 186 High Street is Lenaville, built by prison labour in 1884 for the prison's chief warder, Henry Blinco. George Seddon, Fremantle's Renaissance man, lives there surrounded by a large Mediterranean garden. He lectures Italians in Florence on the Italian garden — in Italian. He's always writing his final book. I find his knowledge about everything is daunting. Next there's Samson House, a boom-style villa built in 1884 with the turret added fifteen years later by Talbot Hobbs. Samson House has a number of interesting features. It is the home of two mayors of Fremantle, Fanny Samson's son Michael, and Michael's son Frederick. For most of his life Frederick slept here in the room in which he was born. On a verandah is Sir Frederick Samson's personal movie theatre with seats salvaged in 1952 from Fremantle's last tram. Freddie Samson's war-time home movies are rated among the world's worst — and most interesting. His house has a deep well cut in the limestone and now covered with heavy glass. Before the 1899 extensions the well was in the back yard. Afghan drivers camp opposite in Fremantle Park. Some water their camels at the Samson well, others at Fremantle Park, before leaving for the Eastern Goldfields. That drink in Fremantle will get them to Northam. The ships of the desert look over square-riggers and the more prosaic steam ships.

Finally you reach the lunatic asylum, built in the 1860s by convicts for crazed convicts. It is now the Fremantle Arts Centre and Museum. It is an agreeable place now but vivid stories of ghost sightings abound. This is not surprising given its varied uses before being rescued from demolition and then restored in 1970: lunatic asylum, girls' home, old women's home, TAFE classroom. Plans for alterations to the building for the US submariners' base show a small room chillingly marked 'gas chamber'. The asylum's gardens become the Fremantle Leisure Centre.

Stroll back through Fremantle Park, diagonally across from the Samson house. In the early 1890s this can be a wild place: the Fremantle Football Club plays its home games there on a stretch of stony grass. It is given by the government to Fremantle in exchange for the Fremantle Green which has been resumed for the original railway station. Matches are no

The Fremantle Lunatic Asylum, completed with convict labour in 1865, before restoration, 1970, and detail of the original shingle roof.
[Michal Lewi]

Fremantle Park, an early football battleground, as seen from a Quarry Street building, c1940.
[Fremantle City Library: Local History Collection]

teddy-bears' picnic. On 18 July 1891 Fremantle plays the Perth Rovers. The game, always violent, ends in a riot although this is not immediately apparent from the typically overblown report in the *Western Mail:*

> *As soon as the game ended a disorderly mob, including many elderly men, surrounded the pavilion and asserted the umpire had behaved with partiality and harshness towards the Fremantle team and had been unusually liberal to Rovers.*

This means that the umpire, William Croft, a former Rovers player, is doused with buckets of water, grabbed by his neck and coat, and thrown against the pavilion wall. He is only 'saved from being killed' by Fremantle players Frederick 'Paddy' Knox, formerly from Norwood in South Australia, and William Augustus Bateman, the acknowledged Father of Football in Western Australia who played the 'Australian Game' at Prince Alfred College in Adelaide.

Meanwhile Harry Marshall, the Essex Street baker, secretary of the Fremantle Lumpers' and the progressive Liberals Association, official of the Fremantle Football and Rowing clubs, and a charismatic larrikin, runs around the ground stirring up the crowd. He shouts, according to the *Western*

The Fremantle Ladies Cycling Club, with the celebrated Cannon Eward Collick (right), sets off near Fremantle Park, c1920.
[Fremantle City Library: Local History Collection]

Samson House, corner of Ord and Ellen streets, 2006.

Mail, 'Bring 'em down and go for 'em. I'll pay the costs.' Mounted police and some players protect umpire Croft from the 'roughs' and finally get him onto the train for Perth. Come Monday and Marshall is paying his own costs in the form of a fine. He is also gaoled for twenty-four hours. A band plays at the prison gates and the crowd cheers when he is released the next day. The more Harry fights at the football the more popular he seems to become, even when Fremantle moves to the more constraining Fremantle Oval. Harry's prominence as a sportsman sees him elected to the Legislative Council seat of West Province, based on Fremantle, in 1894. The *West Australian* is not happy; it calls his election 'a disgrace to the whole colony'. Harry has to campaign from prison as he had, in 1893, been convicted of forgery and given a huge fine, which he cannot pay. There's an irony here, his father Edward had come to Fremantle as a convict with a fifteen years' sentence for forgery. Harry Marshall is declared a bankrupt and his seat declared vacant.

You can follow the path of umpire Croft after the riot by moving down Adelaide Street to High Street then on to the old railway station. On the way you pass between the Catholic basilica of St Patrick and the 150 year old Fremantle Boys School. Across the open space Catholic and state school boys once threw stones at each other until the respective principals staggered the school lunch hours.

The trip back to Fremantle can take you to Kings Square beside the Town Hall. Around dusk you'll see a lean energetic man darting about as he models a head. He wears a suit, as he usually does at work. He is Pietro Porcelli and he's cast in bronze but every time I see him he looks increasingly realistic. Porcelli, who was born in Italy in 1873, becomes one of Fremantle's artistic heroes and a rare early bohemian. His studio is a limestone store with a shingle roof at the rear of 52 Henry Street. Local kids come in to watch the sculptor at work: he seems to like them being there, apart from his unpredictable outbursts of temperament. His rustic fountain in granite and marble commemorating Tom Edwards is also in Kings Square. Bill Latter says the work is done with enthusiasm. 'Porcelli was a socialist,' he tells me and describes some of his memorials after the 1914–18 war. They are more like peace memorials. The C Y O'Connor statue now at the entrance to the port is his best-known work in Fremantle.

Fremantle sculptor Greg James is working late, around midnight, in his studio at the rear of 52 Henry Street. He is grinding-off his Porcelli bronze, without any idea of his studio's very special provenance. It had been Porcelli's studio. The heavy jarrah door opens; visitors often come in from the street to watch a pour. For safety's sake he switches off the

There are several romantic theories for why Pietro Porcelli, the sculptor, signed himself as Peter just once — for a young woman's headstone at Fremantle Cemetery.

[Michal Lewi]

grinder, then looks up. A man wearing a blue cotton smock and baggy woolen pants is watching him. It's Pietro Porcelli. He moves to the workbench and examines closely the bronze sections of his torso. He seems pleased. Then he disappears.

If you can beg, borrow or hire a bike there are many places to which you can ride. For instance White Gum Valley and North Fremantle have collections of small wooden cottages in areas like White Street and there's North Fremantle Oval situated between John Street and the river. Ever wonder what a football ground would be like a hundred years ago? It would be just like North Fremantle Oval although I was surprised that some claim the grandstand was rebuilt after a fire. Planners seem to have been determined to reduce this sliver of land between the river and the Indian Ocean to roads and an accompanying industrial complex. They have failed because of the cohesion of the North Fremantle community.

The ride I like starts from Arthur Head and runs along Marine Terrace, past the water police cottages. You'll ride close to the sites of many of the merchants' town houses, built near their business headquarters — Moore, Samson, Higham, Manning, Bateman, Diamond and Marmion. In 1880 South Bay is yet to be reclaimed. You pass the 888 sign — eight hours work, sleep and play — which is on the 1904 Fremantle Trades

Greg James' sculpture of Pietro Porcelli in Kings Square.
[Greg James]

The old Fremantle Trades Hall has had many more names since this photograph was taken. Note the Paddy Troy seats on the Esplanade Hotel verandah where port casual workers could wait for jobs, c1974.
[Michal Lewi]

Hall, appropriately painted pink. Or I like to think it's pink, not terra cotta. John Forrest, the conservative premier, arrives to lay the foundation stone; the conservative strategist, Joseph Allen, is the architect. The politics of the times are more forgiving than now. The mile-long funeral procession for Tom Edwards leaves from Trades Hall. During the America's Cup defence the Italian syndicate is based here and the Aga Khan sets up a very classy — and expensive — restaurant. Now a brass plate announces it is a reception centre named Esplanade Manor. Across the road, on the verandah of the old Esplanade Hotel, are three benches. They are installed in the 1940s by Paddy Troy for the 'Seagulls', the most casual of casual port workers, those who will take any job. Paddy Troy doesn't like the name Seagulls. Dignity of labour is important. Now at least the dockies can sit and wait for work in some comfort.

You next pass a sequence of short streets leading down to the sea, in an area once known as the Golden Mile. When Kalgoorlie loses its glitter, miners come down to Fremantle and work on the wharf. Then the Italian fishermen move in, first as tenants and later as owners. Suffolk Street has such a history. In the twenties a Sicilian, Savario Pensabene, lives at No. 20. Each morning at two he rolls up his pants to the knees and puts on his cap. He wades to his boat and leaves on the land breeze, heading out past Rottnest. The previous day he will have scattered his craypots, apparently haphazardly, in rough water often thirty fathoms deep. He has no instruments to help him find them and no winch to pull them up when he does. He knows where each pot is: just as he knows precisely where he is if he can just see a speck of the coastline. Capo d'Orlando fishers can do this.

Savario returns with the sea breeze, the well on his boat a mess of scrabbling crayfish. He'll unload them into a large wooden crate suspended beneath 'Dago' Jetty. But, if the local boys haven't already done it for him, he has first to release a number of the crays he caught the day before, equal to the fresh ones he wishes to hold. Fishing is a compulsion — or a therapy. Savario can't stop even though a chaff bag containing ten dozen crays will fetch him only ten shillings — if he's lucky. With no refrigeration and no export market the fishers can't hold out against the buyers. Life gets even tougher during the Second World War but Savario survives internment and the seizure of his boat. He resumes fishing after the war but prices are still low: kids like me use frozen crayfish tails as the bait of choice, at three shillings and six pence for two.

Then America discovers a taste for local crays. Fremantle cray fishermen like Savario become comfortable and even wealthy. Line fishermen have their troubles, with the price of dhufish and snapper, which they catch in deep water off

A freighter aground at
the end of Suffolk Street, 1922.
[Fremantle City Library: Local History Collection]

Savario Pensabene and crew heading for Rottnest.
[John Pensabene]

Following page: The final pour at E and G Foundry (originally Furphy's), 1986. Fremantle once had thirty-eight foundries. The building at 12 Grey Street has now been converted to a sail-maker's loft.
[Fremantle City Library: Local History Collection]

Rottnest, being capped artificially low by the state price controls. In the evenings they net from the shore in front of their houses, hoping to catch herring and garfish. And that is no better financially. The line fishermen may be mostly Italian but they come from two different regions, have different fishing backgrounds, and won't agree on a common push for fair prices. Frustrated, they arrive at the Fremantle Trades Hall, where Paddy Troy acts as an independent arbitrator — and honest bloke. Agreement is reached and the result is the Fishermen's Cooperative and better prices.

Eight years ago, while riding south, you could have been engulfed in a glistening silver, green and white cloud which screeches; a cloud of seagulls. They gather over a fishing boat where sardines are being unloaded into pine boxes on the back of a truck. The truck moves through the city to Jim Mendolia's sardine factory in Beach Street, near where C Y O'Connor's house and stable once were. The seagull cloud moves with the truck. Traffic lights disappear beneath this noisy assemblage until it reaches Jim Mendolia's sardine factory. Sadly the cloud is no more: Jim has moved to Rous Head, once home of Harwood's whaling venture.

You are crossing into South Fremantle, the village within a village. There are smaller numbers of birds all the way to Douro Road. Here they scavenge on a rectangle of grass, defined by South Terrace and the railway line. It is known as the Wilson Reserve but more generally as the Rec (for Recreation). It's a small space. The popular women's cricket team of the mid-1930s occupies part of it. On the rest of the grass, big boys play close, aggressive football. Post-war they will be South stars — Jack Murray, Frank Jenkins, the Lewington brothers Clive and Neal, and Jack 'Corp' Reilly, who seems to be impossible to hurt. 'He's like a crayfish,' says Ron Hart, a small kid. 'His bones are on the outside. You can't hurt him.' State and Catholic school kids still throw stones at one another. Reilly is a convent kid and sits with his pile of rocks in Lefroy Street, beneath the butcher's plate glass window. No-one dares to throw anything at him: they could break the window instead of Corp. The wily kid later becomes an even wilier captain of the red and whites.

We are on the beach years later and Ron Hart tells me about the day Ron Doig died in 1932. Doig is captain-coach of South Fremantle Football Club and captain of the Fremantle cricket team — and a god to the kids. They love his fairness and his grace and that he wears red and white. Ron Doig dies of wounds received in a semi-final the previous afternoon. The kids are playing marbles when the terrible word comes through. Jenkins kicks the marbles away and draws a circle in the ground with his toe. The others follow. What does it all

mean? No-one can say. On the way to the funeral the group notice Fremantle shops are closed for the morning. At Fremantle Cemetery one of the group climbs a tree to get a better view of the grave. He falls through the crowd and into a pile of sand — but no-one even notices. A magpie in a nearby tree chortles. I know old South fans who still pause as they pass 14 Howard Street, where this model of fairness and athletic grace lived with his parents.

You reach South Beach which, in the first half of the twentieth century, is an entertainment centre with big ideas about itself. Fremantle is a resort town in summer, with any spare rooms being rented and tents being pitched in back yards for a small fee. South Beach is the day-trippers' target with pretensions: it calls itself Brighton. One opening day for the summer season sees 35,000 visitors turn up, mostly by train or tram. Frequently, they change on the train, swim in the shark-proof ocean pool and, later, attend what may be the state's first open-air picture theatre. The adults watch the silent movies from deckchairs and kids sit in the sand at the front. There are also vaudeville shows and visitors dance or roller skate at the Hydrodrome, which was a hospital ward built in South Terrace to treat the physical and psychological wrecks of men returning from the First World War. Percy Wright's merry-go-rounds are big attractions and he keeps on building them around the state

Fremantle's women cricketers shared the Rec ground with budding football stars Corp, Scranno, Clive and Jack in the 1930s.
[Fremantle City Library: Local History Collection]

Following page: The old change-rooms at South Beach, with a range of equipment for hire, c1922.
[A Orloff]

Dressing Rooms Ladies 2d
Costumes 6d 3
Towels 2d Caps 3d
Vs Only 2d Lockers 2
All Charges Hour
Gents Lockers 2d
VALUABLES
TAKEN CARE OF
3D.
PARCELS &c 2D
M.J. FIELD

ING ROOMS.
GENTS.

South Beach. Crowds at the end of jetty; and on the grass, with the smelter in the background, c1924.
[A Orloff]

until well into his nineties. The other Percy, Percy Button the escapologist and acrobat with a rupture, is another attraction.

Towering over all this entertainment is the smoke-stack of the Fremantle Smelting Works which extracts gold and other metals from ores brought by rail from all parts of the state. It opens in the early 1900s, employs 400 people and has a tall chimney which sends sulphurous smoke over the beach and Fremantle washing lines. An early report states, seriously: 'It is scarcely possible to imagine a more ideal spot for a smeltering works. It is well-removed from the populous part of the port, although connected with the main railway system by a branch line and stands on an elevated position overlooking the Indian Ocean.' During America's Cup time the twenties were revisited. Steam trains crowded with picnickers ran along that branch line to South Beach while residents objected to the soot on their washing.

In the thirties, things change. The smelter, which prospered during the First World War, roasting Northampton lead ore for the production of artillery shells and bullets, closes. The sea advances and damages the Hydrodrome: the rock wall no longer offers any real protection for the sand and the swimming beaches disappear. A shark appears inside the 'shark proof' baths. The US infantry, which has a camp nearby in 1942, decides the smelter's chimney is too distinctive a navigation guide for enemy submarines and demolishes it in 1942, to the considerable safety concerns of those who live in the dunes, including a number of Nyungars waiting for relatives to be treated at Fremantle Hospital.

South Fremantle is the home of the racehorse and the battler, as well as the swimmer. More than two hundred of the limestone and wooden cottages have had stables out the back. The bigger stables have grand names like Randwick and Sandown. There are local farriers and local kids work as strappers before they go to school — if they go to school. Local hero Shiner Ryan lives in the feed store beside a stable in the fifties and pays his rent by making jiggers (battery-loaded whips) at a small radio shop in Market Street. At dawn horses clip-clop down the streets which lead to the beach. The residents come out to meet them. 'How'll he go on Saturday?' someone asks. 'Good 'orse,' or ''ome and 'osed,' is the set reply. There are shades of meaning in the intonation. The walk down the street and through the dunes is enough to warm up the galloper — and scare anyone sleeping rough after a heavy night — before it is given a hit out on the firm beach sand. That evening the boys who 'ride work' take their girlfriends, who typically live less than two hundred metres away in this tight community, to Mrs Campbell's pie shop at the corner of King

Chesterfield, south of South Fremantle, c1910: little boxes with thunder boxes and horse boxes out the back.
[Fremantle City Library: Local History Collection]

Street scene: Terry Patterson (left), guardian of South Fremantle's horse heritage, helps shoe a locally-trained galloper outside his home at 77 Daly Street, 2006.
[Dianne Davidson]

William Street and South Terrace. The boys eat a threepenny pie; the girls share a milkshake or spider with the boys. There is a strong social order here.

On Saturday the horse train steams off for Ascot or Belmont or Helena Vale or wherever that week's race meeting is held. South Fremantle horses appreciate Helena Vale with its long finishing straight. It reminds them of the long straight beach on which they gallop. The train may carry fifty or sixty horses plus the strappers, who avoid paying their fare by hiding perilously among the nervous legs of the thoroughbreds. Women may put their Royal Ascot finery at risk in the horse-class carriage. Sometimes, the railway inspectors walk by. 'Anyone in there?' they'd call. 'Only us horses,' would come the reply. I think I've heard the same story about chickens in a black-American version, but Mick Vodanovich, entertainer, hotel keeper and 'Fremantle's Michael Edgley', swears it happened.

When the horse train returns on a New Year's evening, the Perth Cup winner may stomp down the ramp. Watchers clap and reach out to pat their champion. Then he walks home to further cheers and has a celebratory chomp or kick at the weatherboard walls of his stall. Meanwhile the local kids search the train for empty beer bottles, worth all of a halfpenny each. Some of them will ride in an annual event on South Beach for horses of a different size — the Draughthorse Derby. Cartage

The Collinson racing stable on Daly Street, c1940, now owned by an unhappy Terry Patterson. He says: 'Once people came out to greet the race horses; now they try to get rid of them.'

[Fremantle City Library: Local History Collection]

contractor Bartholomew Timothy 'Bat' Daly runs Clydesdale races, with kids riding bareback or using a pair of seven-pound flour bags stuffed with straw for a saddle. Daly's stables still line Hulbert Street where they serve as an electrical contractor's workshop. On the other Sundays of the year, kids take the horses down Douro Road, then hose them down when they return. The beautiful Daly house, built from wood, is at No. 15, and is now a bed and breakfast establishment — with a spa.

You'll be riding close to a significant piece of Fremantle history at 1 Walker Street, just south of Douro Road. No.1 is the three-room weatherboard cottage where Len Lewington lives. The first of the Lewingtons, William, arrived in Fremantle in the first three months of the colony. He was a lively bricklayer and gravedigger who often seemed to be heading for a duel with his father-in-law who was unhappy with his daughter's choice of husband. Len likes the stories about his forbear. Len has lived in his present house since he was five, which is a long time, since he was born in 1913 in a semi-detached just a couple of doors down the street. Len's house is a lived-in museum. Nothing changes. The scrubbed-pine kitchen table is where John Curtin plans his election campaigns for the seat of Fremantle (which includes conservative suburbs like Cottesloe and Claremont) in the twenties and

John Curtin opens South Beach summer season, 1928.
[John Curtin Prime Ministerial Library]

thirties. Len's father Tommy, the longest serving member of the Australian Labor Party at the time, and Alex McCallum, the member for South Fremantle and Deputy Premier, meet him there. They dispatch Len to paste flyers on power poles advertising that Curtin's rallies will be held at selected street corners and conducted from the back of a truck. Come into the front of the cottage. This is his brother's racing bike in the hallway. The brother was a state champion. Here is Len's original iron bed. Here is a photograph of Len's sister who was a champion runner and cricketer; and here are photos of his cousins Neal and Clive Lewington, both captains of South Fremantle Football Club, who grew up nearby, and here's a list of the family members who played for the two Fremantle teams. It is a long list.

Len is a small assertive man who wears his red-and-white South Fremantle beanie with pride, and talks in fractured sentences about his time as a union rep at Pearse Brothers boot factory. But he is loud and his meaning is clear. He likes to tell you how he outfought an American contender for the world lightweight title who was stationed in a camp near his house on the Rec nearby. The pair had a disagreement. Until his eyes packed up recently, Len would ride his bright green bike into the city. Once every two years he paints his heritage-listed house in maroon and yellow. He's having trouble when I meet him. 'The bleedin' parrots have eaten all me almonds and I can't do anything to stop them. They won't let me fire my shotgun around here any more,' he complains. The 'bleedin' parrots' are massive black cockatoos which fly down to Fremantle from the Murdoch University campus. The sky darkens as they drift across any yard with an almond tree. I come back that afternoon to conduct an interview on John Curtin. The large tree has been chopped down and Len is working on the stump. 'Well the bloody parrots won't get any more of my almonds,' he says as he puts his axe away. Nor will anyone else.

Len devotes more than twenty years to a busy campaign to get public recognition in Fremantle for his friend from Fremantle Boys School and South Fremantle Football Club, Air Commander Sir Hughie Edwards VC, KCMG, CB, DSO, OBE, DFC, Equerry to the Queen. But after twenty years he has nothing to show for it: not a picture, or a bench, nothing at all. 'Perhaps I would have done better if Hughie had been an Italian,' he laments as he points to a dozen newspaper clippings, skewered on a nail in the kitchen wall. Ron Hart, a historian of Fremantle football and particularly of the Doig family, tells me of the controversy among friends when Hughie leaves Burt Street Army Barracks, where he is a Coastal Defence Corps gunner, to enter the pilot officer training

Len Lewington, 2006, sitting at the kitchen table where his father and John Curtin planned election stategies. A plaque on this heritage cottage reads: Owner Len Lewington; designer Len Lewington; restorer Len Lewington.
[Michel Lewi / Aaron Photographics]

Davilak Hotel, South Terrace, 1905, before the trams arrived. The coach (left) was operated by the Collins family, who also built Len Lewington's cottage.
[Fremantle City Library: Local History Collection]

Following page: Like an industrial cathedral: the old South Fremantle Power Station.
[Sophie Van Der Leeden]

school at Point Cook. Is this the right thing for a White Gum Valley boy to do? Different people had different views. Ron also mentions a similar conflict faced by Frank 'Scranno' Jenkins, his Beaconsfield Primary School classmate and one of Fremantle football's greatest, when he is offered a foreman's job on the wharf soon after the Second World War. It means more money but also joining 'them' and leaving 'us'. Scranno couldn't do it, even though Emelda Day, a trusted influence on South players, said he should. Ron and I are standing on the Rec ground where he played football with Scranno. He says he is uncomfortable telling these stories. He is a Beaconsfield boy who lives in Cottesloe and works as a inspector with the Australian Tax Office. He says that when Hughie Edwards was State Governor, he told him that his six games with South Fremantle were the most significant moments of his life.

More recently, powerful people push for a memorial to Sir Hughie Edwards. Soon a larger-than-life bronze of Sir Hughie, his eyes looking skyward waiting for the last bomber to return, is unveiled at Kings Square. The RAAF turns on a fly-over, complete with 'bomb blast' manoeuvres. Some sponsors carry more influence than Len.

You are now riding through Fremantle's back yard, and against the wind. You always seem to have the wind in your face as the cycle track winds through spinifex-covered dunes.

It's a spectacular, wild ride even though you are only three or four kilometres from the city. The crushed bodies of billions of sea urchins have coloured the sand an unexpected grey. Ahead is an industrial cathedral, the decommissioned South Fremantle Power Station. The interior is covered with vividly coloured erotic fantasies painted by a team of not untalented graffiti artists. They are also good at climbing fences.

You pass a valley near the Catherine Point groyne. In the valley was a place called Hollywood, a camp for Fremantle's aspirational drunks. Hollywood residents live in cottages made from packing cases and flattened tin salvaged from the local tip. They use paint tins for their pot plants and grow pelargoniums along their shack walls, hence the occasional pelargonium still showing its head above the sand at the camp site. Friends come from other camps to holiday there, I'm told. But they are a different class of resident from those at the Smelters Camp or nearby Beverly Hills, which is a suburb of Hollywood and attracts the real outcasts. A strong sense of irony must have guided some unofficial nomenclature committee. Those at Beverly Hills made a little money digging and sifting shell grit which they dry on the beach before bagging it. Everyone has chooks. The Beverly Hills grit means harder shells on eggs from Fremantle chooks fed on wheat which was probably brought home from the wharf in a lumper's billy.

In the sea beyond Catherine Point there's a monument of a symbolic rider and horse, by Fremantle sculptor Tony Jones. On 10 March 1902, C Y O'Connor, the creative genius of the Goldfields Pipeline, rides from his home in Beach Street and on past his new harbour. He is alone, as his usual partner on these morning rides, his youngest daughter, is sick. He is severely depressed after continuing criticism of his integrity and competence. He rides into the water and shoots himself in the mouth — but not before he removes his dentures and places them in his pocket.

Nearby in the dunes is another monument, to the colony's first horse race in 1833. It is called the Horse Memorial and is a wire sculpture of the scene by North Fremantle sculptor Anne Neil. Seven Timor ponies are lining up across the beach seeking a generous five sovereign purse. Lionel Samson's horse, wryly named More In Sorrow Than In Anger, is unplaced.

Before Robb Jetty is built — and afterwards, as a measure against Kimberley cattle tick — long-horned bush bulls are pushed from their ship down a slippery ramp and forced to swim ashore. A character called 'Wingie' protects them from large tiger sharks which, if the one-armed rifleman is on song, will soon be boiled down for their oil at the nearby Shark Factory.

Tony Jones' sculpture with cattle cutouts and a crush, enig-

C Y O'Connor memorial
by Tony Jones.
[Tony Jones]

Tony Jones' sculpture
The Human Race.
[Tony Jones]

Landing cattle at Robb Jetty, c1920.
[Fremantle City Library: Local History Collection]

matically called the Human Race, crosses the cycle track and leads to the cattle paddock and then on to the killing chamber. It is a compelling piece of interpretation, but not all bulls readily accept the fate organised for them. Some head for Fremantle.

Margaret Sloss tells me of her encounter with escaped north-west bulls. She was born in 1902 and lived in Hulbert Street in a three-room corrugated iron cottage, built hard against a sand dune, for almost ninety years. She is one of ten children: they had to sleep four to a bed. They are poor but, like other residents in Hulbert Street, they don't pay water rates. The man who lives in Hulbert Street's 'big house' works for the water authority. He sees that records for water users in the street are 'lost'.

Margaret was returning home with classmates from Beaconsfield Primary School and walking up a steep sandhill when three Robb Jetty stockmen came galloping up the other side. The celebrated Aboriginal stockman, Wandi, shouts: 'Get back to school. The bulls are loose.' The kids are on their way, except for Margaret who becomes entangled in a barbed wire fence. She watches the long-horned beasts approach her at speed. Then the stockmen turn them.

I decide to walk back along Hampton Road — the track often taken by runaway bulls eighty years earlier. I find myself in a chaotic collection of small trade and metal fabrication workshops. In one is Robbie Lang, designer, steelworker, proponent of 'jazz architecture', philosopher of materials. He's a Scot, obviously; happy among rolls of reject steel, and what he calls 'found objects' which he admits to sometimes making. Everywhere there are gates and screens featuring curving metal, wild but under control. It's easy to recognise his work in cafes along the coffee strip. He wants to free up people's design processes so they can 'create beyond their ability.' Robbie tells me he is from Greenock in Scotland where great ships are built along the Firth of Clyde. Greenock dies as a ship builder when Robbie is a teenager, on his way to becoming a marine engineer like his father, his grandfather, and his uncle. At fifteen Robbie wins a scholarship with IBM and is taken through their extraordinary production processes. It is, he says, an 'apprenticeship in alchemy.' He is at Silicon Valley at twenty where his job is to keep the processes of computer chip manufacture running. He also explores US scrap yards filled with large cars. Then he looks for a home where there's a sense of community and the sun shines. He comes to Fremantle, which in one way reminds him of Greenock. Both have a community but Greenock hasn't much sun. And jazz architecture? It involves capturing the moment; a lack of formal planning; improvisation; and lots more.

Mail men outside South Fremantle Post Office, Hampton Road, c1896.
[Fremantle City Library: Local History Collection]

The last day on the Mills and Ware Swiss-roll assemby line, 1991.
[Fremantle City Library: Local History Collection]

I leave Robbie to his welding. I am now riding in South Terrace. South Fremantle has changed. Twenty-five years ago it was notable for cheap rents and anti-nuclear campaigners, and of course Mills and Ware. Now it features eats and arts and its old houses have become expensive. Opposite the converted Mills and Ware's factory I talk with Andrea Pruneddu at La Vespa Patisserie. Andrea is a fourth generation cake-maker and has arrived from Sardinia. His cakes, like his country of origin, are a blend of Italian and French tastes and are irresistible, especially the raspberry mousse. The naming of his shop coincides with a surge in ownership of Vespa motor scooters in Fremantle. The cake shop used to be the Family Butcher, which was run by an Italian for forty years, and retains traces of its past in the butcher rails hanging from the ceiling. In an even earlier incarnation the shop belonged to one of the five generations of Sowdens who were butchers in Fremantle, the first coming off the Long Jetty in 1890 and walking south with his family to find a house in Orient Street. La Vespa has become a meeting place for 'old South Fremantle types'. John Troy hosts a table of lefties most Saturday mornings.

A hundred metres down the street is the Fremantle Contemporary Art Gallery and studio of Elizabeth Mavrick who manufactures shimmering, changing, fused glass wall panels. Elizabeth, who grew up in Fremantle, used to be a potter but discovered her true art form a decade ago and has now established an international reputation. A visit to the Kimberley eight years ago resulted in her work getting larger and her colours changing. I first visit the gallery with Cecile Dorward, nearly six feet tall when she was almost ninety. She is an expressive woman. She looks at Elizabeth then at a panel: 'But you're so little. But very good.' Elizabeth says this is a common response.

Soon I am strolling in the High Street Mall wondering about the essence of Fremantle. The Mall is a different world from that of the Strip. It's older and poorer but not sadder. Culley's Tearooms is there, where at 3.30 each afternoon the leftovers drop to half-price: scones 25 cents. The facade of the Majestic Theatre is almost immediately opposite and I recall Thelma Limpus's comments about the theatre's stunning white marble staircase and what it was like for a ten-year-old in the 1920s to walk down it. (Thelma Limpus was, incidentally, a Fremantle chiropodist and podiatrist for fifty years.) My stream of consciousness takes over again. I remember stories of Black Paddy, the Robb Jetty stockman with the infectious laugh. He would sit in the front row of the Majestic and constantly laugh. The laughter would spread until everyone was laughing. Try to find the Majestic

La Vespa Patisserie, once a butcher's shop, 2006. Note the photo exhibition of Indian sacred cows on the meat rail.
[Aaron Photographics]

Following page: Installing tram power cables, c1905.
[Fremantle City Library: Local History Collection]

facade. A clue: look at the exposed ironwork.

Once more I am walking along Market Street, the street which has never included a market. Now there are no butchers or supermarkets; not even a fish shop. The old fish shop becomes The Old Fish Shop and sells china. Then it sells souvenirs. The butchers, who specialise in real veal, say rents are too high and leave about America's Cup time. The footpath is busy — like High Street forty years ago. I'm moving past tables where diners are eating wood-fired pizzas or cafe food piled on lots of sprouts or Fremantle sardines which I remember as my old tailor bait, mulies. I don't recognise anyone. I remember the courtly old men from the Imperial Bedrooms who used to cross South Terrace to get their three thick slices of Italian bread, a dish of butter and a bowl of chicken noodle soup at the Capri. The cost is ten cents or nothing. They come early to free the tables for those who arrive later to eat squid grilled over a large wood stove, or boiled crayfish. The old men are gone and the Imperial Bedrooms are no more. The Capri is still the Capri.

I am now heading for the wharf. Commercial and warehouse buildings are becoming residential: the oyster-openers' building in Pakenham Street has been converted into residential units. Lads with oyster-shaped calluses on their palms not so long ago sold bags of sixty or seventy slightly

Royal Photo Co
No 1
MUNICIPAL TRAMWAYS

CLEARWAY
C
NO STANDING
CANTONMENT

STATION
HIGH
Cut 14 yea
off your home
Nation

Fremantle street scenes:
Notre Dame students and old friends,
Fremantle Harmony Week, 2003.
[Antoinette Van Der Leeden / Lusia Rensmaag]

Previous page: a tanker crosses Market Street.
[Photo Moderne]

battered oysters for $5, for those with a special taste in stews. Is something lost when industrial buildings are converted to housing? Some think there is. Is there an alternative? Well, yes. High Street between Market and Pakenham has acquired four fashion shops since I last had a careful look. Love in Tokyo, Deep Odyssey, Kellie Rose and Hustle are keeping eleven designers busy. Further west, towards the Round House, are further fashion shops with names like Poets of the Machine. In a dozen out-the-back rooms, which once housed kids from Greek and Italian families, stocks from shops and hardware stores, churns from milk-bars and scraps from cafes and butchers, are silks and satins and people sewing and models sneaking an early try-on. I pass groups of tall African students from the University of Notre Dame. At the wharf an old Italian man sits on a rusty bollard, gripping a length of Rangoon cane to which three metres of line is tied. He can't stop fishing; the habit of a lifetime. He throws in handfuls of burley from a plastic bucket. Large skipjack come to the surface and are expertly flicked on to the wharf with this primitive rod. The skippy are intercepted on their trip to intercept the especially sweet king prawns swimming through the tidal swirls beneath the traffic bridge. They are large prawns and heading for the ocean. Ted Lewis, ninety-six and one of the original Wharf Rats of the local oral history book title (produced by Fremantle

Primary School), still has a prawn which is 24 centimetres long, preserved in methylated spirits for the last seventy years. I'm told bigger prawns have been netted, up to 30 centimetres.

As a kid, Ted and his friends would gather wheat from the wharf and take it in tins to the old bridge. As a ferry passes beneath the kids call to the passengers who, looking up, are showered with wheat. When the police appear at one end of the bridge the kids high-tail it down the other. One day the police approach from both ends: 'Caught like a wharf rat in a trap,' Ted mutters.

I notice few are working on the wharf where once there would have been hundreds. When Americans loading their submarines in 1944 showed Fremantle lumpers a primitive forklift, the locals didn't realise that this would be one of the weapons of their destruction. Then in 1969 the first container ship, *Encounter Bay*, berths. End of story. Look around the harbour. Even the ships don't look like proper ships any more; more like tall boxes with a pointed end and drop-sides across which Japanese cars speed away. They are much bigger than the old cargo vessels. I wonder how these transports manage to float. Three people separately tell me that things are not the same since the Patrick's stevedoring company attempt to install their own non-union workers: that two of Patrick's men fought on North Wharf over the forklift which could unload the most cargo

The fate of 2000 lumpers was sealed with the arrival in 1969 of the first container ship.
[Fremantle Ports]

containers per hour and thus earn one of them more money.

A Sims Metal ship ties up. She looks more like a proper ship. Dump bins filled with scrap metal are tipped into the open holds. It's an interesting clatter for some. A resident in a new development in North Fremantle rings Fremantle Ports to complain about 'all that noise at 5.00am when people should be asleep'. Perhaps there's a crushed Renault 12 or Peugeot 504, which were once the popular Fremantle second-hand cars, among the metal being loaded. There are now more Renault Clios and Peugeot 336s in Fremantle streets than the old favourites; perhaps even more Porsches and BMWs. I notice a sign screwed into the limestone at 1 Mouat Street — Rolls Royce. Is this another pointer to Fremantle affluence? Or has Rolls Royce sent its agents to find and destroy the 1930s RR which the Deputy Mayor, Denis Sowden, cut down to a utility for use in his butchering business. 'It's very reliable for deliveries,' he says in the 1980s. I enter the office. A polite man comes to the counter. 'We're the Marine Division. Twenty thousand ships have Rolls Royce parts in their propulsion systems. No, we don't sell cars here.' There's an old horse trough outside. Next door is a homoeopath. That's a Fremantle touch. Rolls Royce is part of Notre Dame next time I pass.

Number 5 Mouat is constructed in the Federation Romanesque style in 1903 and leased to L Rattazzi and Co, the

The Tarantella, 5 Mouat Street, c1975.
[Michal Lewi]

This Nairn Street terrace is looking the worse for wear in the 1970s — as is the boarder on the balcony, right.
[Michal Lewi]

Imperial German Consul and agent for Norrdeutscher-Lloyd Imperial German Mail Steamers. It's an obvious centrepiece for anti-German rumours during the First World War. Is Rattazzi spying on ship movements from his top window? There's no evidence for it, although the building does look a little sinister. The conservation architect, Ian Molyneux, describes it as 'a highly individualistic and rugged building; quite brutalistic.' As the Tarantella Night Club in the seventies and eighties, the building is all of those things. It is port life in the raw. There were syringes in the street, midnight sex being vigorously and noisily transacted over car bonnets, angry adjoining residents, and inside there's a metal strippers' cage painted red. Is it to protect the strippers from the patrons or vice versa? The Tarantella next houses Notre Dame's School of Medicine. It may see blood and syringes again but in a different context.

Nearby I encounter an old acquaintance who always tells me how Alan Bond saved Fremantle by winning the America's Cup. I always tell her that Fremantle was a wonderful place before 1986; that perhaps its large warehouses were 'underused' by artists but were filled with creative energy. Yes, post-1986 there were gains; these were exciting times. But there were also losses. Jack Wynhoff's garage, which stretched between Collie and Nairn Streets, becomes an accountant's office. Jack has kept a fleet of Renaults and Peugeots running around Fremantle with his acute ear for engine problems, spare parts from wrecks in his Nairn Street backyard and a piece of cord to check wheel alignments. Academic and architect, Geoffrey London, who lives opposite, wonders how he will start his Peugeot on cold mornings without Jack. Jack says he presented Geoffrey with a particularly heavy hammer with which to hit the jammed starter motor. The drunks who convert any open space around Nairn Street into an unofficial parking area and provide an informal security service for residents, get short shrift and also go. I meet Nigel, a picture framer from Bitches Brew, outside the darkened P and O Hotel. We talk about hotel closures. He tells me he is not a big drinker but a closed bar door reminds him of the teeth of a snarling dog. We notice some workers' clubs are struggling.

I wonder whether it's true that this wonderful, picaresque town has sunk beneath the weight of what some irreverent residents call Catholics and the weekend ice-cream lickers? Is Fremantle no longer the place where Fremantle people live, at least during the weekends? Sam Abercrombie is painting in Portugal; Nunzio has found himself less than comfortable with big money restaurant operations and opened a popular Italian restaurant in Bali, but is now back and just recently acquired the old Roma. Bill McKenzie and Bill Latter and Connie Herbert and Victor Gubgub are all dead. But some of the old

The Cleopatra Hotel, c1988, became the Auld Mug Tavern for the America's Cup; it is now the Edmund Rice (Social Justice) Centre.
[Brian Richards]

Strand Cafe, 49 Market Street — 'Best Meals in Town!' and 'Take Home One Dozen Oysters for 1/6,' they advertised, c1940.
[Saxon Fogarty]

Fremantle survives: like a dislike of suits. In the 2005 Fremantle City Council elections the top end of town endorses two candidates who are pictured wearing suits in their advertisements. They get hammered. 'Never trust a man who wears a suit,' says a correspondent to the local paper.

Many who grew up in Fremantle and couldn't get out quickly enough now want to return. The price tags — up to $1.6 million for a unit in an old North Fremantle shipbuilding yard — retard them. I remember one of Henry Briggs' early houses, a two-storey Georgian dwelling in Ellen Street being sold for $22,000 in 1974. It was sold recently for $1.45 million. Does all this make Fremantle boring? I ask Margaret McPherson, specialist nurse and history graduate from Murdoch University, what's left of the old Fremantle: 'Not much. Only Bousfields (the century-old clothing store in High Street). Even the Italian studs have disappeared from South Terrace.' When Margaret began nursing at Fremantle Hospital in the 1950s the down-and-outers from the Smelters Camp or Beverly Hills were admitted at Christmas for a few days' respite from their hard lives. The holiday season was a time when there were spare beds at the hospital and the unhappy campers came in for a clean bed, Christmas dinner and some TLC.

I call by Lance Holt School in Henry Street. Lance Holt was Western Australia's first community school and dates back to

Lance Holt
Community School, 2006.
[Lance Holt Community School]

the early 1970s. There's a Fremantle feel about the place. It's International Peace Day and the kids are writing poems about peace. 'Peace tastes like rocket/fresh from the garden,' writes Sean, age five. An eight year old is more prosaic, he tells me it is good to go to a school which was once a lolly factory.

Development on the Lance Holt site has a timeline similar to many Fremantle blocks. There were two stone houses there in the 1840s, and a shop and a confectioner's in the 1880s; the Federal Coffee Lounge was built in 1892 at the start of the gold rush boom. The building was a warehouse holding jams during the Second World War, then housed a printer before being bought by Main Roads for its Henry Street highway project.

Children from Fremantle Primary School, on the site of the old Alma Street Cemetery, are also in town on a project which reminds me of Larry Foley's interest in contemporary smells. The kids decide the ocean, coffee and sheep trucks provide the town's dominant smells.

I move on. I ask prize-winning novelist Joan London who lives just off the cappuccino strip what's special about Fremantle: 'Everything! I loved it as soon as I saw it.' And why wouldn't she, with a hundred year old fig tree drooping over a side fence, loaded with sensuous, black figs bursting open? Anne Brake first met Fremantle in 1994 when she came here as curator at the decommissioned Fremantle Prison and now lives in a converted pipe factory in North Fremantle: 'It's like a country town. People care about each other and are passionate about their town.' Anne grew up in a small town in northern Queensland.

There's little doubt about the passion. The public meeting is a Fremantle art form. The richly decorated Town Hall is packed for debate on topics ranging from heritage to the frequency of bin collections. 'I come here wearing two hats,' announces one politician. 'And two faces,' interjects someone in the crowd. The prediction that Fremantle is being gentrified to a point where it becomes a conservative electorate shows no sign of happening. Leftish topics like welfare, refugees, Aboriginal land rights, social justice, the bid to save Ningaloo Reef in the state's far north-west (a cause backed by author and local resident Tim Winton), the Republic, and the Greens all have strong support. More esoteric issues are argued, like whether the spectacular 'spaghetti mansions' of the seventies should qualify for a Fremantle heritage bonus. Twenty years ago nuclear disarmament was the big issue.

New Fremantle has many vegetarians. Customers like the way Kakulas Sister in Market Street sells pulses and flours and a variety of dry goods from sacks and appreciate the name which pokes fun at the male chauvinism of Perth's Kakulas

Inside Kakulas Sister,
Market Street, 2006.
[Aaron Photographics]

Brothers. The Perth business started in Fremantle with a fruit stall outside the Fremantle Station. Business is falling away as the Depression bites. Tinny Thomas offers Evangelos Kakulas one of his stalls, at 185 William Street in Perth, north of the railway, providing he also promotes Tinny's secret-formula ginger and hop beer. It is an offer he does not refuse. Kakulas Brothers is still at No. 185.

I ask Mick Vodanovich about the new Fremantle. 'It's a foreign country,' he says. 'Everyone used to help one another.' When his dad, who ran Jack Vodanovich Taxis, heard of the death of a citizen he'd ring the family to offer a 'couple of free cars for the funeral'. Mick is a pub keeper and a showman. He took over His Majesty's Hotel, which he called His Lordship's Larder after the original building on the site. He wanted this tough pub to be a place where judges, workers, priests, nuns, sex workers, actors, architects and acrobats could all feel comfortable together. There must be no swearing. Mick plays the saxophone and Hazel Jones, nudging eighty, is on the piano. Bastille Day is a big hit. So is the corned beef and onion sauce, arguably the best meal in town, along with the prawns. But not even Mick could make the profits needed by the hotel's owners who had invested heavily in its restoration. So Fremantle's Michael Edgley went to the Federal, now Rosie O'Grady's. He invented green beer for St Patrick's Day and brought the

Mick Vodanovich with a pony at the front bar.
[Daniel Bruyn]

Fremantle's Irish arrive at St Patrick's for the funeral of hotelier and patriarch Daniel Mulcahy, 1908. The impact of the Fremantle Irish was great in hotels (on both sides of the bar), trade unions, wakes and religion.
[Fremantle City Library: Local History Collection]

Barmaids' Picnic noisily back to town. The pub was packed — and his rent trebled. He left, saddened. Mick may see Fremantle as another country but he waits in neighbouring Spearwood for his chance to return. When I last spoke with him, he'd been waiting seven years but says it may not be long now.

Fremantle is still the town of special funerals — C Y O'Connor, William Marmion, Tom Edwards, Ron Doig, Bon Scott from AC/DC (in secret), Jack Tonkin … Maybe funerals best represent the essence of the city. I'm thinking about this while attending Stan Lenton's funeral. Stan is the son of Stan Poole, who was captain of South Fremantle in 1940. Like Ron Doig, he is a South captain who dies after being injured in a game of football. Young Stan never sees his father. He works at many jobs and is eventually Fremantle's City Treasurer when the City buys a number of Henry Street properties, which are at risk. Then he becomes a hotel keeper although his playing of Mahler in the Fremantle Hotel's front bar is not altogether successful. Stan moves to the Railway Hotel in North Fremantle, a century old single-storey pub, and resists the state government's attempts to run a railway line through it. The Railway opens at six for those coming off night shift, or are just thirsty early; and it serves a seriously huge breakfast for $6 for those who are hungry as well as thirsty. The Railway is Fremantle's truckies' and wharfies' pub. It attracts some surprising others.

Stan dies of leukaemia. On the day of the funeral truckies on their way to the container wharf slow down as they pass the Railway Hotel and sound their earth-shattering horns. Later there is a line of 40-wheelers with containers parked on the verge opposite Fremantle Cemetery. The mayor is there, major industrialists, barmaids, and men in shorts and steel-capped boots. The funeral closes with Bach. I ask my neighbour David Phillips why Stan was a special and unlikely pub keeper. 'He was always the gentleman. He'd never leave a newcomer to drink alone. And he was a good businessman,' says David who is a violinist in the Western Australia Symphony Orchestra. Soon Fremantle Ports buy the Railway.

The argument about Fremantle and change will continue. For some at least, the significant things don't change. I meet Jack Kent, the international prize-winning architect of resort hotels, who lives in a small weatherboard cottage in North Fremantle. He is standing beside one of the original low stone boundary walls in Henry Street, near his office in the Union Stores building. I ask what he remembers most vividly about Fremantle from the fifties when he would come from Mosman Park to visit a school friend: 'A Culley's cream bun.' And what is the essence of today's Fremantle? 'I'd have to still give the same answer — a Culley's cream bun.' Some things don't change.

'Mandrake' leads the Fremantle Festival parade, 1995.
[Daniel Bruyn]

Following page: High Street, looking west, 7.10am on a summer's morning.
[Michal Lewi]

A Select Bibliography

Bosworth, Michal, *Convict Fremantle: a Place of Promise and Punishment*, University of Western Australia Press, Nedlands, 2004.

Brown, Patricia, *The Merchant Princes of Fremantle*, University of Western Australia Press, Nedlands, 1996.

Dowson, John, *Old Fremantle: Photographs* 1850–1950, University of Western Australia Press, Nedlands, 2003.

Herbert, Xavier, *Disturbing Element*, Cheshire, Melbourne, 1963.

Hitchcock, J K, *The History of Fremantle*, S H Lamb, Perth, 1929.

Hoffman, Louise and Jeffery, Chris, *Izzy Orloff Photographer*, Fremantle Arts Centre Press, Fremantle, 1989.

Lang, Karen and Newman, Jan, *Wharf Rats*, Fremantle Primary School P and C, Fremantle, 2004.

McIntyre, Stuart, *Militant: the Life and Times of Paddy Troy*, Allen and Unwin, St Leonards, 1984.

Moore, George Fletcher, *Diary of Ten Years of an Early Settler in Western Australia*, University of Western Australia Press, Nedlands, 1978.

Reece, R and Pascoe, R, *A Place of Consequence: a Pictorial Guide to Fremantle*, Fremantle Arts Centre Press, Fremantle, 1983.

Acknowledgements

Shake a tree in Fremantle and a master storyteller drops out. Some of the best of them helped me comprehensively with this book: Larry Foley, Connie Herbert, Emelda Day, Alec Smith, Bill Latter, Ron Hart, Ken Hopkins, Mick Vodanovich, John Troy, Jamelia Gubgub and Rusty Christensen are just some of them. Sadly, Bill, Connie, Ron, Ken and Emelda are now no longer with us. But thanks, wherever you are.

Similarly Fremantle has long been a photographer's delight. Renee Hirsch and Veronica Stratton, the devoted nieces of two of the best of them, A 'Izzy' Orloff and Saxon Fogarty respectively, were wonderfully generous with the vast photographic record of their uncles. Michal Lewi was unstinting with his evocative photographs of Fremantle architecture — which incidentally helped protect some of those buildings in the seventies — and with his time in taking new shots recently. Thanks also to current photographers Andy from Aaron Photographics, Jean-Pierre Héricher of Photo Moderne, Brian Richards, Danny Bruyn, Brad Rimmer, Antoinette and Sophie Van Der Leeden, Lusia Rensmaag, Martin Webster and Michael Wearne and the *Fremantle Herald*. Alison Bauer and Loretta O'Reilly, from the Fremantle City Library's wonderful Local History Collection, and Fremantle Ports' Alan Pearce, helped in so many ways; likewise Helen Kirkbride.

First published 2007 by
FREMANTLE ARTS CENTRE PRESS
25 Quarry Street, Fremantle
(PO Box 158, North Fremantle 6159)
Western Australia.
www.fremantlepress.com.au

Consultant Editor Ray Coffey
Cover Designer Tracey Gibbs
Printed by Everbest Printing Company, China.

National Library of Australia
Cataloguing-in-publication data

Davidson, Ron, 1936– .
Fremantle impressions.

ISBN 9 7 81863 683838 (hbk).
ISBN 1 863683 83 6 (hbk).

1. Fremantle (W.A.) — History.
2. Fremantle (W.A.) —
Pictorial works. I. Title.

994.11